ORDINARY PEOPLE,
Extraordinary TIMES

A MEMOIR OF ONE CITIZEN ACTIVIST

LOIS ANN NICOLAI

This book is dedicated to my three granddaughters—

Elizabeth (Libby) Graver

Sophia Graver

Carly Graver-Carnovale

who spent their time, money, and effort to promote the publishing of my first book.

I also wish to dedicate this book to my friends—

Tom Bieg, Carl Bottomley, Zac Carnovale, Connie and Dave Collin,

Carolyn Creamer, Michael Creamer, Gordon and Nori Douglas,

Barbara Fracassi-Nodine, Patty and Townsend Graver, Sasha Herman, Dolores Hewitt-O'Neill,

Cindy Hubeny-Joyce, Tracy Brown

Carol Ann Junker-Bradford, Rich Kaloostian, Walt Muehling, Stella Murashkina,

Jean Dorgan-Nostrand, Marina Puznukhova, Joyce Schweers, and Judy and George Youngerman

Who contributed to the publishing of my book, and who now comprise my "advisory committee."

CHAPTER INDEX

INTRODUCTION

If anyone had ever told me, when I was eight years old, that my life would become such an exciting adventure, I would have probably responded with, "Now that's the life I've been dreaming of ever since I was born!" To me, life was always one big adventure. It just seemed natural to squeeze the most out of everything – from swimming in Noe Pond, with a dozen cows wading on one side of the lily-pad waterhole and us on the other side, to riding my horse, Montana, through the cow pastures around my house or down Green Village Road on my way out to the trails in Meyersville and Mendham. The 40s and 50s were fantastic years to grow up in rural Chatham Township. Life was so simple, and so safe! Our family got our first ten-party telephone line that hung securely on the kitchen wall when I was around seven, and our first TV (with a four-inch square screen) when I was ten. And those first few years, there were four channels that worked from 8 am to 11 pm only, showing the same movie over and over again! From birth until high school, our choices were to read, help with the housework, or head for the outdoors. Needless to say, my domain was mowing the grass, feeding the chickens, weeding and hoeing our garden, cleaning the horse stall in our barn, pitching hay in our hayfield, or helping our neighbors, Mr. and Mrs. Pickle, milk their cow or churn the butter as the three of us sat in their kitchen drinking warm, fresh buttermilk together! Could life be any better than that?

Ten years as a Girl Scout, four years of 4-H, and every sport open to girls were my social life, and I loved every minute of them all. I was even lucky enough to live across the street from Billy and Sonny Behre, so they called me over to their ball field whenever they were a player short, playing baseball and (you're right) football! One highlight of those years was raising my Seeing Eye German shepherd, Karen, before she went into training at the new Seeing Eye Dog Training Center in Morristown. As my inner philosophy developed, I grew to believe that we humans are sent here by God with a distinct mission. By the time I was thirty, I was fully convinced that my mission was to raise my six children, and together survive the Indiana cornfields where we spent eleven summers detasseling Pioneer Seed corn.

But the Lord moves in mysterious ways, and two weeks before five of my children were to return from their summer break to Indiana State University in Terre Haute, my husband of twenty-six years died unexpectedly – leaving me, at forty-six years old, totally devastated.

Once my children returned to Indiana State, I made the decision to head back home to New Jersey. I had come to terms with the fact that my whole life was about to change. I decided to settle on the Jersey Shore and eventually brought all my children here after their school year ended. I spent the next three years walking the boardwalk and beach every morning before work. My vision of a new life soon became a work in progress, ever changing as the sandy shoreline along the Spring Lake and Sea Girt Beach, where I made the magical, difficult transformation of self-discovery, leading me to extraordinary changes. At my fiftieth birthday dinner, I announced to my bewildered children that I was moving to Princeton to become actively involved in International Relations and Peacemaking, to make my contribution toward building a safer and better world for them and my future grandchildren. I believe that was the first time in my life I can remember all six kids totally speechless! As they sat around that lovely dinner table at the Breakers in Spring Lake, I could almost hear their minds' wheels grinding as my news registered: *Okay, mom, Princeton is only an hour away so we can visit – once in a while. You can get a nice little apartment and you'll be so busy you'll never miss us. Meanwhile, we can now live our newfound lives without checking in with you daily anymore. Sounds like a great plan mom!* Thus, they won their new freedom of not answering to me anymore and I finally won mine back!

Professor Richard Falk invited me to stay in his home for a month over the Xmas holidays while he traveled to Israel to testify in a treason trial, giving me a month to find an apartment and a new job. From that moment on, it was like God and His Angels laid out the steppingstones in front of me as I walked my new path. Everything happened at such a pace that it was like one gigantic dream!

From meeting Martin Sheen at the Aquinas Institute, where he chose to sponsor me on the thirty-day Soviet-American Peace Walk across America with 215 Soviet citizens as a result of the growing perestroika and glasnost movement within the USSR in the summer of 1988; doing my first civil disobedience at the Nevada Nuclear Test site in 1989 with hundreds of others; joining the bridges for Peace Exchange with Volgograd, Russia, for a two-week visit, living in the homes of our new Russian host families; meeting with First Lady Hillary Rodham Clinton in the Blue Room of the White House in 1990 before I flew to Reykjavik, Iceland, and spent an hour with the first woman President of Iceland, Vigdís Finnbogadóttir; becoming close friends with Honorable Olzhas Suleimenov, the People's

Deputy representing Kazakhstan in the Supreme Soviet Kremlin in Moscow, as we both worked with the parliamentarians for Global Action nuclear project; traveling to Semipalatinsk, Kazakhstan, in the fall of 1991 at the invitation of Honorable Suleimenov for the official closing of the Soviet Nuclear Test site, where we celebrated with thousands of Kazakh Nomads in the dessert sun before sharing their national meal and drink (fermented horse milk, yah!) with the mayor and his delegation in a gorgeous yurt; to receiving a telephone call *"from the Kremlin"* in early 1992 where Olzhas' translator, Vladimir Iakimets, informed me that Olzhas wanted to send him and seven Kazakh citizens to the United States and asked me to take them across the country to attend the demonstrations at the Nevada Nuclear Test site where they could dialogue with American activists.

One of them was Karipbek Kuyukov, a twenty-four-year-old radiation victim born in the Semipalatinsk Region with no arms. He became famous by painting with a paintbrush in his teeth. After planning the entire trip, I rented a ten-passenger van and drove from Princeton through Las Vegas, where we spent three days dialoguing with Casey Kassem, Daniel Ellsberg, the Berrigan Brothers, and many other activists of those times, to San Francisco and back on a twenty-eight-day speaking tour. The day we returned, we met with the filming crew and news commentator for the McNeil/Lehrer Newshour TV show in NYC and they interviewed my Kazakh friends. A month later the segment was aired worldwide, and soon President Bush announced the Nevada Nuclear Test site would be permanently closed! Underground testing in the USA finally ended in September 1992.

I met with President Nazarbayev in the fall of 1992 at the gala fundraising event and spent an hour in the office of Kazakhstan's First Lady, Sara Nazarbayeva, after presenting them with a $60,000 gift of life-saving medicine donated by Bristol-Myers Squibb for the Kazakh Children's Hospital being built specifically for their children suffering from leukemia caused by the radiation from their nuclear testing; worked side-by-side in 1996 with Costa Rica's former President Rodrigo Carazo and U.N. Under-Secretary General Robert Mueller at the U.N. University for Peace in Costa Rica, where I organized and conducted a three-day seminar with twelve men and twelve women from fourteen countries as we created the "Peace 2000 Initiative"; and organized and drove the 1997 Peace Caravan through Canada, Alaska and back across the USA—and the 1998 Peace Caravan from Calais, France, through Europe to the Norwegian Mountain Range from Oslo, Norway, to Jokk Mokk, Sweden, north of the Arctic Circle, where we spent a week eating reindeer meat cooked a dozen different ways. Within my Peugeot Boxer van, I transported four Indonesian professors from Muhammadiyah University in Jakarta, Indonesia, four nuclear activists from Almaty, Kazakhstan, one Cree Indian from Alberta, Canada, and one other American. During each ten-week trip we lived with host families in all twenty towns we visited, where we held dialogue seminars, many times attended by more than a hundred local citizens.

I was also sent by the U.S. State Dept. from 1997 through 2012 to serve as an OSCE/PAE International Supervisor and Election Officer running the first democratic elections in Bosnia-Herzegovina, Kosovo, Serbia, Macedonia, Croatia, Moldova, and Soviet Georgia, and my last mission in Siberia in northern Kazakhstan.

However, out of all my excursions, the next two are most dear to my heart. Why? Because my best friend traveled with me. Rose Marie Tucker and I hung out occasionally as high school classmates, but once we graduated, we went our separate ways for almost forty years. In 1992, I sent out an invitation to all my former high school classmates, inviting them to join us in Princeton at an open house for our newly formed 501(c)(3) organization, World Citizen Diplomats, and Rose Marie showed up! She joined our growing group of peacemakers that evening and became an active member and soon a close friend. In 1993, I was putting another trip together to visit my new friends in Kazakhstan and Rose Marie and another member, Charlotte, decided to join me. Charlotte had been traveling all her life but had never been to Uzbekistan, so I agreed to ask my friends to obtain visas for us so we could go down to Samarkand, not far from the Afghanistan border. This is an incredible story, but unfortunately there is not enough time to share here. You will have to read my second memoir, which should come out soon! (I'm working on it.) I will tell you that my friends could not acquire the visas for us, so they strongly advised me not to go into Uzbekistan without a visa. Unfortunately, I gave into my crazy friend Charlotte, who insisted we absolutely had to go anyway! My Kazakh friend, Umyt, was furious, but she allowed her husband, Zhamil, to escort us as our translator and they hired a driver who was a frequent visitor in Uzbekistan and knew the police and roads. Umyt and Zhamil knew the danger of Americans traveling without visas in these underdeveloped Asian nations and knew how bad the prisons were in their part of the world. All I can say is, we are safely home in America because of Zhamil and our driver. All the police were corrupt and stood out on the road stopping each car without Uzbek license plates to take every nickel from every outsider. Not only did they get all our American Dollars and Soviet Rubles, but all of Charlotte's British Pounds too. Thank God, Umyt made us leave most of our money at home with her. The only reason they didn't arrest us and throw us in jail is because we gave them everything except the clothes off our back, and Zhamil and our driver talked them out of it! But we did make it to Samarkand, and it was unbelievable. I closed my eyes while standing on the cobblestone street, and honestly felt I might see Jesus walking by – in other words, it was just like it probably looked 2,000 years ago! It was truly breathtaking.

In 1999, Rose Marie and I headed out again, this time to the Hague in Netherlands, where we spent a week participating in the Hague Appeal for Peace Conference. There were almost 10,000 peacemakers there, representing every country of the world. We had our World Citizen Diplomats Booth and held a two-hour seminar for many to participate in. This was the hundredth anniversary of the first World Peace Conference held in 1899. There are a lot of good people all over the world trying to make their contribution for a better more peaceful planet. It is a terrific crowd to be among!

How could I ever have been so fortunate and blessed to live a more fulfilling life than even my childhood dreams could imagine? Today, you need to be much more cautious of where you venture, but my message to you is to do whatever your heart is telling you to do. Follow your intuition and dreams but do it when the time is right in your life. I now know my first mission was to raise my children, and all that knowledge I acquired growing up in Chatham Township and raising a little army in Indiana taught me so much that came in good use when I started my international work. Don't think for one minute you aren't qualified because you're not rich, or famous, or beautiful, or well educated enough, or that you're too old! I was none of those things (well, maybe a little on the old side), but I listened to my inner voice and just made myself available!

Once I returned home in 2002 from my second six-month assignment in Kosovo, I settled on the Jersey Shore and started writing my memoirs.

My first book, *Ordinary People, Extraordinary Times: A Memoir of One Citizen Activist* is this book that you are about to read. It has all my missions focusing on my nuclear disarmament work as a citizen activist.

My second book, *Ordinary People, Extraordinary Deeds: A Memoir of a World Citizen Diplomat*, is being written now. It tells the stories of all my citizen diplomacy trips abroad, the two ten-week peace caravans, (the first in the USA and Canada and the second throughout ten countries in Europe), the Soviet-American Peace Walk across the USA and many international seminars.

My final book, *Ordinary People, Extraordinary Lives: A Memoir of One American Family*, will soon follow. It opens in 1740 when my four Fleming Brothers Ancestors arrived in the USA from Northern Ireland with their wives and first children, settled in the remote western New Jersey, built their tavern/home – which they named Fleming's Castle – and founded Flemington, NJ. It is the story of my ancestors, my growing up years in Chatham Township, NJ, and the twenty-six years I spent raising my family in St. Paul, IN.

I hope you enjoy this first memoir and look forward to my second one to be available soon. Enjoy!

CHAPTER 1

RETURNING HOME TO NEW JERSEY

I spent the first twenty-six years of my adult life as a housewife in the American farmland surrounding Saint Paul, Indiana, where my husband and I raised our six children. After he died unexpectedly on August 8, 1983, my children and I clung to each other for a short time, coping with our grief and shock. Everything happened at such a fast pace. We soon made the arrangements for Jim's funeral, which was held one week following his death, when I realized the children had to pack and return to Indiana State University. Our lives had to move on despite our loss.

Only two weeks after his death, on August 21, the younger five of my six children left for their autumn term at Indiana State. In just two weeks' time, my home, which I shared with my husband and younger five children, emptied—leaving me feeling alone and lonely.

I spent the next four months getting my children settled at school and closing the house we lived in. We all spent the Christmas holiday in Terre Haute, which turned out to be one of the coldest winters in history. It was −64 degrees below zero wind chill factor on Christmas Eve, closing Christmas Eve midnight mass services.

On January 2, 1984, I packed my car with whatever possessions fit and gave every piece of furniture to my son Michael and his fiancée, Angie – who now had an apartment in Terre Haute – and my daughter Eileen and I headed east. Eileen had made up her mind that she would pursue a dancing career, and she wanted to study under Luigi in NYC. We moved in with my parents, where I grew up, in Chatham Township, New Jersey. That winter I enjoyed getting to know them on an adult level, because I married and left home when I was only twenty years old. After spending the winter with them, Eileen and I made the decision to settle on the Jersey Shore. During all those years in land-locked Indiana, I grew to miss the ocean almost as much as I missed my parents.

In early May, Eileen and I drove along the Jersey coastline. I told her, "Eileen, let's look for a safe little community to settle in. You girls have practically lived your whole lives in Saint Paul, Indiana. I'm not sure if it's considered a village or a town, since it has less than a thousand people and is more than twelve miles from the nearest town, but it offers a very safe environment to raise you kids in. As you can see, New Jersey offers a whole different life from the Midwest."

"Mom, we're more streetwise than you give us credit for. Remember, we've all been living at college in Terre Haute the past few years, and it's a much larger town than we grew up in. But I agree that a small community would be nice," Eileen responded.

"I hope we can settle close to the ocean so we can spend lots of time on the beach and boardwalk, but I'm certain it's expensive. We'll have to agree on very small accommodations for the summer," I told her.

"That's fine with me. Wherever we live, I'm sure it'll beat our dorm room at college," Eileen remarked. At that, we continued our drive along the shoreline, laughing and bursting with anticipation and excitement. As we drove south along the coastline, we pulled into each little beach town and evaluated what we liked and disliked.

When we arrived in Spring Lake, we drove along the boardwalk overlooking the beach; then we viewed all the shops along Main Street; we drove around the lake and observed the magnificent Saint Catherine Catholic Church on the south side; and we gazed in amazement at all the gorgeous homes and bed & breakfasts. It didn't take us very long to decide this would be our first home on the Jersey Shore.

I telephoned my other children at Indiana State and asked them to join Eileen and me as soon as their spring semester ended. Brenda immediately agreed to come, but Patty put her foot down. "I'll come to New Jersey and visit for two weeks, but no longer. I plan to go back home to Indiana, so don't you dare beg me to stay any longer. You know I HATE New Jersey."

Michael was now engaged to his college sweetheart, Angie. He, Angie, and my youngest son, Jim, chose to remain in Terre Haute and continue with summer school. Debbie, my eldest daughter, was raising her three children in Greenfield, Indiana.

Having been born and raised in the cornfields of Indiana, my children hated visiting New Jersey. All they remembered was the traffic and pollution. We never had the opportunity to spend more than a few hours at the beach during our short visits, so they had no idea what the Jersey Shore was all about. I knew they were soon in for one of the biggest and best surprises of their lives.

Patty and Brenda arrived on a gorgeous sunny morning in the third week of May. Eileen and I had already moved into a lovely large room on the second floor of a bed & breakfast, five blocks from the ocean. It had four beds, lots of dresser drawers, and a big spacious closet. We even had our own private bath attached to our room. It was an elegantly furnished room and when the girls saw it, they dropped their suitcases and jumped up and down with joy.

Eileen took the girls out to experience the nightlife each evening and to the beach every day. On the fifth morning, Patty looked across the breakfast table and said, "I love the Jersey Shore. I'll never go back to Indiana." Thus, three of my daughters were hooked!

All four of us had no problem finding waitress jobs. Eating establishments along the Jersey Shore were hiring daily in preparation for the "100 days of summer" officially beginning on Memorial Day and ending on Labor Day.

We lived in that one big room from May until September, saving every penny possible. In September, we were able to find a year-round rental for $1,200 a month. It was a lovely four-bedroom home in the center of Spring Lake. We split the rent four ways, paying $300 each, and agreed to split the utilities and groceries too. We joined Saint Catherine's Church where I was soon proudly singing in their superb choir. Our new life on the Jersey Shore had officially begun.

That next spring my eldest daughter, Debbie, allowed me to drive out to Indiana and bring her and my three small grandchildren back to New Jersey to visit with us over Easter. After a few days of experiencing the nightlife each evening and the beach every day, she too was hooked on to the Jersey Shore. Debbie had been a single mom for a few years now, working hard to raise her children. She liked the idea of being close to her family again and she, too, had never experienced the Jersey Shore, which she later found exciting. To top it all off, in that first week here, she met her future husband who lived in Sea Girt.

Finally, I had my four daughters and all my grandchildren here with me. Michael and Angie were married that summer and they stayed with Jim in Terre Haute to continue studying at the university.

The next few years I walked the Spring Lake and Sea Girt beaches each morning, watching the sun rise and searching my soul with one big question. What was I going to do with the second half of my life? I loved going to the beach early in the morning before anyone arrived, enjoying the solitude of just God, His ocean and me. I felt closest to God at the water's edge, smelling the salty ocean air and feeling the fresh sea breeze on my skin. I loved the sound of the seagulls as they playfully flew overhead. Sometimes I would sit in the sand near the water and just watch the breakers flow in and out and the seagulls play tag in the sand. The sound of small two-engine airplanes flying overhead was exhilarating. It brought back memories from my childhood when I would lie flat on the ground in the high grass covering the hill next to our lily-pod pond behind my house and watch the small airplanes fly overhead. I couldn't wait to fly in one someday. The sounds and smells by the sea brought me such an amazing feeling of peace. Any stress I might have had before arriving at the beach disappeared. It was as if my soul had been cleansed. What an incredible way to start my day.

My awakening didn't happen overnight. I walked the beach every day possible, during all four seasons. In the winter, when it was too cold to walk on the sand, I would sit in my parked car on the road in Sea Girt overlooking the beach, with my heater blaring on high and all my windows wide open so I could hear the mesmerizing sounds. This went on from the fall of 1984 until the spring of 1987 – two-and-a-half years.

My thoughts were filled with memories of my twenty-six years in Indiana. Oh, how I missed my husband. It took a long time to come to terms with his untimely death. I believed all my life that everything happens for a reason and has a divine purpose, but it was a long struggle accepting his death.

I thought a lot about my work as a Mary Kay Beauty Consultant. I worked part-time with Mary Kay, both in Indiana and New Jersey for more than seven years. Now I finally had ten recruits. I was on my way to becoming a Mary Kay Director and driving my own company pink Cadillac.

But then the questions started to surface. To take director status, I would have to work many more hours. If I worked hard, I would be able to buy a nice home with a big dining room where I could entertain my children and grandchildren for holidays and Sunday dinners. I thought about the commitment it would take to purchase a home at fifty years old. I would have to pay a mortgage every month until I was eighty! I'd have to clean the house every week or pay someone to clean it for me. I would have the expense of utilities and upkeep both inside and outside.

Then I thought about my daughters who were dating their future spouses. It wouldn't be long before they would buy their first homes and surely, they would want to take turns hosting our family gatherings.

Soon it became apparent to me that I really didn't need or want a big house of my own. I'd become a slave to my new home and all its expenses, and yet I'd be living alone, with no extra money or time to enjoy the second half of my life. Now I was more confused than ever.

Finally, very early one gorgeous morning in April, I was sitting on a rock on the jetty overlooking the majestic sea. I finally thought to myself, "Lois, if you were diagnosed with a terminal disease and the doctor said you only had one year left to live, what would you want to do in that last year?" I began exploring every possible option and finally concluded that I would want to do something to help leave the world a better and safer place for my children and grand-children. Once in focus, it was that simple.

During my growing up years, I had always been interested in people throughout the world. Therefore, it didn't surprise me when I finally made the decision where I would go from here. At my fiftieth birthday dinner in April 1987, I announced to my bewildered children that I planned to move to a university town to learn everything I could about international relations and peacemaking. The result of those years walking the beach searching my soul as to what I wanted to do helped me decide to make my contribution for a better world.

In early December, I walked into the Registration Office at Princeton University and asked the two ladies at the desk, "May I please pick up a schedule of your night classes in International Relations and Peacemaking?" The two ladies looked at each other in amazement and then turned to me as the older lady said, "I'm sorry young lady, but this is an Ivy League university and we don't have night classes here. You might wish to inquire at a community college." Obviously, my years in the Indiana farmland hadn't prepared me for "Ivy League" status.

"Oh, I'm sorry, I didn't realize that. I'm planning to move to Princeton and wish to become involved in international peacemaking. Would you have any idea whom I should speak with?" I asked. The ladies recommended talking to Professor Richard Falk, the university's leading peacemaker and Director of the Woodrow Wilson School of Public & International Politics.

I found his office and asked June, his secretary, if I could see the professor. She explained that Professor Falk was getting ready for his next class. "Would it be possible for me to sit in on his class?" I asked.

"Well, truthfully it isn't done very often, but I don't believe there is any rule against you observing his class," she said. I thanked her and found my way downstairs to the classrooms of the Woodrow Wilson School. I sat in the hall and watched as the university students filed into their classes, and then I walked into Professor Falk's classroom. I introduced myself and asked if I could sit against the wall and observe, and he said yes with a little bit of a surprised look on his face. There were fourteen students in his class, representing at least ten countries. It was so exciting listening to discussions between students from so many different cultures and nationalities.

After class, I asked Professor Falk if he had time to talk. He apologized. He had a faculty meeting immediately following the class but asked if I could come back on Wednesday between two and four o'clock.

Of course, I was there the next Wednesday at the stroke of two. June ushered me back to his private office and told me to "just go in." Unbelievable! I found his office packed floor to ceiling with books. I made my way around the maze as I called out, "Professor Falk?"

"I'm right here," he called back.

I finally found the desk where he sat, with more piles of books that extended from the top of his desk to the ceiling. I'd never seen so many books scattered around one room in my whole life. At least in a library they are stacked neatly on shelves. I could not imagine how he found anything in that mess.

"Hello, Professor Falk. My name is Lois Nicolai and I would like to talk to you for a few minutes, if you have the time."

For the next forty-five minutes, we talked. I found him to be an amazing man. He impressed me as the perfect senior fellow at an Ivy League University. Approaching sixty, with gray hair and beard, he had a warm smile and witty personality. I sat mesmerized as I listened to his knowledge of world affairs. We also shared a little about our personal lives and I found him to be very easy to talk with. He told me that he was divorced, and his ex-wife was a psychiatrist in New York City. I told him I wanted to move to Princeton and get involved in social and environmental issues and learn about peacemaking and international relations. I said I had to find a job and a place to live, but I was determined to make the move as soon as possible.

"Well, Lois, you are certainly welcome to move into my home until you find an apartment for yourself. I'm leaving in a few days for the Middle East where I'm testifying in a trial for a young man who was one of my students here. He has been accused of treason back in his own country of Israel and I will speak on his behalf. Since we are off from classes for the next three weeks over the Christmas holiday, I will be gone until January 10. My home is yours to enjoy, and that gives you a good three weeks to find a job and an apartment."

"Oh, Professor Falk, that's wonderful. You are so generous. This way I can move over in the next couple of days and I'll be all settled by the time you return. Thank you so much."

In my excitement, I practically fell over a pile of books as I scrambled to my feet and shook his hand. As I turned to find my way out through the maze, Professor Falk called after me. "Oh, by the way, Lois, would it be possible for you to check on my son, Noah, every so often while I'm gone? He's sixteen and doesn't want to accompany me on my trip this time. He would be thrilled if he could remain at home, and you needn't worry about him. He takes good care of himself."

"Of course," I quickly agreed, still excited about moving to Princeton and beginning my new adventures. I drove back to the shore and packed my suitcase, heading off to Princeton in December 1987. I was as excited as a teenager leaving for her first semester of college. I was certain my new life in Princeton was part of my destiny!

Two days before Professor Falk left for his trip, he greeted me as I arrived at his front door. He led me into his living room where I dropped my suitcases and stood in disbelief. Never in my life had I ever believed someone could actually own thousands and thousands of books. In every room of his home, all three floors with six bedrooms and four bathrooms, were wall-to-wall built-in bookcases piled with thick books. No matter where you stood or sat or ate, you felt the urge to reach out and pull a book off a shelf to start reading. Television never came into your mind in this house.

I totally forgot what a sixteen-year-old could do in three weeks without a chaperone. I am still forgiving Richard Falk for his trickery. I found out from neighbors and storekeepers that Professor Falk had gone through every lady in Princeton over the years to watch his menace. The first few days went by comfortably enough and I found Noah to be quite enjoyable and easy to converse with. One Friday, I was out all day looking for my new employment and decided to enjoy an early dinner at a lovely local restaurant. After dinner, I drove back to Richard's home on Prospect Street at about 5:30 pm as the winter streetlights were just flickering on.

As I approached my destination, I could not believe my eyes. All three floors of the house had lights on in every room, and four or five kids stood out on the balconies of the second and third floors each. As I parked my car, I could hear music blaring from every open window in the house, and I could hear explosions of loud talking and laughter.

"Oh my God," I thought to myself. "This looks like a scene from 'Animal House.'" I opened the front door and found the entire first floor thick with young people. And the stench! Even though I never used drugs myself I knew instantly that the smell had to be a foreign substance. There wasn't a kid without a drink in his hand, and I doubt any one of them was over seventeen. I ran throughout the first floor looking for Noah, but no Noah could be found. I ran up the staircase to the second floor and opened each room, finding kids in every possible situation – doing everything imaginable. Still no Noah! I ran up to the third floor and finally found Noah in his bedroom with a dozen other guys. "Noah, what is going on here?" I screamed. He smiled as I approached him and said not to worry because his dad didn't mind if he had some friends over. "Noah, there must be 200 kids in this house. All underage, drinking and using drugs! This is absolutely unacceptable," I yelled. "I want every person out of this house NOW. Not in five or ten minutes, but NOW."

Unfortunately, I could see from his expression that he wasn't a bit impressed with my insistence. I told him I was calling the police if everyone wasn't gone in five minutes. When I stood there with my hands on my hips waiting for everyone to vacate the room, Noah finally got the message that I meant business.

But ten minutes later, there were still more than a dozen kids in the house, so I telephoned Richard at his residence in Israel, because this was before people carried international cell phones. I told him the situation and he said to me in his mild-mannered voice, "Lois, please let me speak to my son."

When Noah finished talking to Richard, he handed me the phone. "Lois, I'm so sorry. I told Noah he is to put every person out of our house immediately and he is to clean every room tonight and tomorrow. I also told him he is not to have more than two people at the house at any given time. If he doesn't do as I said, please call me back," Richard said. I thanked him and hung up.

Other than having to call him twice in Israel during that three-week period, I made it through the experience without a nervous breakdown. By the time January 10 rolled around, I was moved into my own little apartment on Spring Street and had found a job.

Once settled, I started creating a plan, deciding how I would begin this new phase of my life. I attended lectures and seminars on International Relations at the university. I joined the Coalition for Nuclear Disarmament, where I began learning about the hazards of nuclear radiation. I volunteered for every opportunity that came my way to learn everything I could and possibly absorb all that was going on all over the world.

Within a couple of months, I met my first Russian friend, Dr. Elaina Ershova, who was a research scientist at the USA–Canadian Institute for Peace in Moscow. Cora Weise, the director of SANE/FREEZE in New York City, asked me to plan an itinerary and take Elaina on a week- long speaking tour throughout New Jersey and Pennsylvania. Thank goodness for those twenty-six years of experience in Indiana organizing scout troops, summer day camp, PTO in our school, and the girls softball team, building and developing my organizational skills.

I arranged the whole week with two or three gatherings a day. Many of them were with the National Organization of Women Voters, and others with various peace groups. I drove her in my car, giving us lots of time to talk. On the fifth night, I had organized a dinner in her honor, which was held at Professor Falk's home. He and I invited fifty professors and media to attend, and after dinner, we sat around the living room for two hours while Dr. Ershova answered questions.

This was 1988 and communism was still fully intact. These professors were thrilled to have the opportunity to pick the brain of an active Russian scientist, and Elaina could not have enjoyed it more.

The following day while I drove to the next speaking engagement, I confided in Elaina. "Last night, I sat on the fireplace hearth listening to all the professors asking you about your work in Russia and it dawned on me that I was the only person in that room without a PhD. How can I acquire the respect of my academic friends when I only have one year of college? How can I get them to take my work seriously without a university degree? I am seriously considering going back to college to get my diploma."

"Lois, the world is full of professors writing reports, magazine articles, and books on global problems, but what really is needed are people willing to work, communicate, mobilize and involve others in action. This important work is what you do best, and the world needs you desperately to do it."

It was this conversation that motivated me to begin my peace-making years as an organizer and activist.

My five younger children the day they returned for their fall
semester at Indiana State University, Terre Haute.

Top: Dr. Elaina Ershova (far right) with me (red jacket), <u>Bottom</u>: Professor Richard Falk

CHAPTER 2

MY FIRST CIVIL DISOBEDIENCE

Today is April 14, 1989, and as I celebrate my fifty-second birthday, I'm preparing myself psychologically to encounter my strongest commitment to date in my new work as an active peacemaker. I am making my first contribution to help free our world of the threat of nuclear annihilation by demonstrating against the testing of nuclear weapons going on at the American test site in Nevada.

Last night, I was among the fourteen representatives of the Princeton Coalition for Nuclear Disarmament who bade farewell to our families at the public library on Witherspoon Street and set off for the Philadelphia airport. We were flying to Las Vegas, NV, with much more serious intentions than most people who go there to enjoy the casinos and sunshine of the Nevada desert. Once on board, I comfortably sat back in my seat with my eyes closed and recalled the words of Margaret Mead who said: *Never doubt that a small group of thoughtful, committed citizens can change the world. Indeed, it's the only thing that ever has.*

Several hours later after getting settled at our hotel and catching a few hours of sleep, we ate a late breakfast and headed out to the entrance of the Nevada nuclear test site. As we approached the gate, we saw the city of Mercury, off limits to the public. This city represents the government expenditure of more than fifty cents of every dollar we pay in government taxes. This outrageous spending is used for war preparation and nuclear testing. Only .02 cents of every dollar go into housing in our country. And even more disturbing, only .02 cents goes toward education here in the United States.

Tomorrow, we will perform Civil Disobedience with more than a thousand American citizens from every walk of life and many from several foreign countries worldwide. We are all here to participate in a nonviolent resistance to what we call our government's "Taxation for Annihilation." We want nuclear testing stopped now, and the land returned to the rightful owner, the Shoshone Indian Nation.

Two months ago, on February 19, Friar Richard Rohr and 110 others were arrested on this spot for nonviolent civil disobedience. Their arrest was the culmination of the Franciscan weekend portion of the Lenten Desert Experience's forty days of prayer and protesting nuclear weapons testing in the Nevada desert. More than 400 Franciscan brothers, sisters, and friends came to Las Vegas for this event. Friar Rohr characterized the 1980s as "the decade of denial," which saw the continual progress of the military economy preparing for war while insisting they were preparing for peace. The Franciscan weekend came following earlier Ash Wednesday actions led by Father Daniel Berrigan, Bishops Gumbelton and Buswell, and Archbishop Hunthausen. There was also a seminarian weekend with theologian Mary Hunt as the featured speaker. These Lenten Desert events were sponsored by the Nevada Desert Experience, a faith-based organization resisting nuclear weapons testing.

Much to the surprise of most of us here in the eastern part of the United States, such demonstrations are going on continuously. I spoke to many New Jersey residents, both before I left for Nevada and after I returned from participating in the events. None were aware that our country was still testing nuclear weapons – an example of how the media hides what the government wants hidden.

Across the main road from the entrance to the city of Mercury is the Peace Camp, erected by a group called the American Peace Test (APT). As we looked out over the Peace Camp, I saw hundreds of tents and people of all ages. Driving into the camp, I noticed that everyone was very friendly and relaxed. Every person was here for the same purpose, to become educated on the health hazards of nuclear radiation and to speak out against the nuclear testing.

When we signed up at the registration desk allowing us to participate in the following day's events, an officer of the Western Shoshone Nation greeted us and presented a permit allowing us to enter their land. Thousands of square miles of this land were taken from the Shoshone Indians in the 1950s so the United States Government could stage nuclear testing on it and hide their secrets in the forbidden city of Mercury. Naturally, the Shoshone Nation wants its land back, which, of course, the United States Government refuses.

Some of the members of our group will camp here tonight, so we all went out into the desert and helped them pitch their tents. Tomorrow we will join them to attend the big Peace Rally before we participate in the resistance.

A little before 10 am the next morning, we approached the Peace Camp. We were shocked to see hundreds of cars, vans and buses lining the road. Reporters stated that more than 3,000 people showed up for this one day of events. During the two-hour rally, many people spoke from the stage that was built specifically for this event. One woman, Barbara Wiedner from Sacramento, CA, who founded "Grandmothers for Peace" in 1982, shared with us what members of her organization are doing to help rid the world of nuclear arms. Their statement of action is everything I believe every grandparent wants.

After the speeches ended, we began to line up along the barbed-wire fence that surrounded the nuclear test site. Of course, the testing is done several miles inside the premises, so we couldn't see the holes or areas where the testing takes place. Nuclear testing started in the 1940s and 1950s above ground, but gradually there was a global agreement signed by the five nuclear powers to move all testing underground when it was realized how much radiation was released into the air. But even underground testing vents lots of radiation into the air and pollutes all the ground water for hundreds of miles around the site.

Our group of fourteen men and women from New Jersey stood with arms around each other in a tight-knit circle. Led by Bob Moore, we shared a short moment of silent prayer before moving into our place at the line along the fence. Bob is the minister of a small Christian church in Princeton, and he is also the director of the Coalition for Nuclear Disarmament (CND). As the organizer of this trip to Las Vegas, he was the one who encouraged me to participate. The CND was the first organization I joined in January 1988, when I was searching for a way to become involved in the peace movement.

The line of human bodies was more than a mile long. When the loud signal was given, those of us who chose to commit this act of civil disobedience crawled under the barbed-wire fence. Eight of our group were among them, and the other six were witnesses to the act. Those who stayed behind were our support group, which we were more than grateful for.

Yes, I was one of the eight who actually committed civil disobedience. I'm sure my mother and father would have said it was far from the first time I was ever disobedient. However, this was a very intense and important time for me. Before coming to Nevada, I looked up the definition of "civil disobedience" in the dictionary and found it to be "passive resistance." That sounded easy enough. I knew I could certainly do this with a snap of the finger – or so I thought. So why did I feel so breathless suddenly? I had been preparing for this day for a month now, with absolutely no reservations. I believed in the cause and felt a strong desire to express my feelings against the testing once I began learning the harmful effects of radiation. Here I was, spreading the barbed wire with the help of two witnesses. At fifty-two years old, I was the "old lady" of our little group from New Jersey, although up to now I had no trouble keeping up with the younger members. The first leg went through fine, but I couldn't get the second leg through easily and soon my pants were caught on the barbed wire. My friends helped loosen me and I fell over into a ball on the other side. Because I had been jogging almost daily, I was in excellent physical shape, so I scrambled to my feet and brushed off the sand. When the eight of us were ready, we held hands and walked out into the grounds of the "no trespassing" land, singing *We Shall Overcome* as we approached the guards standing in front of us, preparing for our arrest.

As we walked, and as I tried as hard as I could to sing, my voice choked with emotion. All I could think of was how important it is right now to speak out against this terrible threat. How thankful I am to live right now, at this moment in the history of all humanity, when what I do and what I stand for can help create a better world. If I believe in it strongly enough and if I work at it hard enough, I believe I can help rid the world of these horrible bombs. If God had given my soul the chance to choose when I wanted to come and spend time on His beautiful planet Earth, I would have begged Him to send me when the people of the world wanted peace badly enough to create it. I believe now is that time. My one wish is that every human being soon realizes how fortunate we are to have an opportunity to pull together in creating the one thing every person of all time ever really wanted – peace on earth – without the threat of nuclear annihilation!

Suddenly, I became overwhelmed. As I looked around on both sides of us there were hundreds of men, women, and teenagers all struggling with this same emotion. Some were running as fast as they could toward the test site with one or two guards chasing frantically after them; some were lying on the ground rolling over and over trying not to be contained and handcuffed; some were sitting on the ground praying; some were crying out loud and screaming that the guards didn't understand what they were doing by being a part of the government's war machine; others were laughing as the guard put the cuffs on them.

As our line approached, one guard put his hand up and shouted, "That is as far as you are going!" We stood frozen in a little line, just the eight of us, as the guards walked along and placed the handcuffs on each of us, one by one. They told us to walk toward the fenced-in holding areas, while hundreds of our supporters on the other side cheered and clapped as we stumbled in a single file with our hands cuffed. Many of my fellow captives, those with their hands cuffed in front of them, held their hands in the air, smiling and cheering. They were very proud to have done what they came here to do. But I didn't smile. I felt good that I had chosen to be here, and I wanted those on the other side of the fence to know I was very serious about what I was doing. But what I never expected began to happen. I could feel tears rolling down my cheeks. And since my handcuffs had my hands tied behind my back, I couldn't even wipe them off. Soon my whole face was flooded with tears. When the people on the other side of the fence saw my face, many of them began to cry too. I'm not sure they knew that mine were tears of joy. There was so much emotion swirling in the air that day.

Back in May 1988, I attended the Philadelphia SANE/FREEZE annual dinner. I witnessed Dr. Benjamin Spock receiving the SANE/FREEZE Peace Award and listened to him as he described how he chose to speak out through civil disobedience in the late 50s and 60s. He told how he was almost tried for treason with Daniel Ellsberg, who released the pentagon papers exposing the government cover-up of the Vietnam war. That was when I knew I would have my say someday too. My conviction is that it is never too late to do what you believe in, and I grew up always speaking out with my opinion. Now freedom seemed more important than ever. Thanks to my courageous parents, who allowed me to live my life as a free spirit, I have never been afraid to speak my true feelings. Thank God I was born in America. I have learned that freedom of thought, word, and deed does not exist everywhere. But if you believe in freedom in your heart, no one can take that away.

When we arrived at the holding area, which was an immense fenced-in yard with a dividing wall in the middle to separate the men from the women, we were searched and stripped of anything other than our clothing. They took my peace pins off my shirt and took my jug of water. We had been coached ahead of time not to bring any ID or money, because it would all be confiscated. It was almost hundred degrees and our holding area was entirely in the sun, so the water concerned me. However, once inside, I saw several large containers of water available. No cups, though, so we had to drink from the palms of our hands, losing half the life-saving water through the space between our fingers.

Once I was settled inside my prison, I remained near the entrance so I could observe everything going on. I was impressed by the attitude and behavior of most of the officers. There had to be somewhere between fifty and seventy-five men and women officers, although most of them were women. Most of these women were members of the Nevada State Police, and a few were United States Marshals. They were built like the amazons I read about in comic books when I was a kid. Their bodies were in perfect shape, uniforms starched and pressed with pleats, and boots that looked new and perfectly shined. You could tell they were very proud of who they were, and they appeared to be professional and pleasant. Most of the men were also well-groomed and well-mannered. But I did see one nasty hothead who cut the wrists of a lady when handcuffing her after he was forced to chase after her out into the desert. She looked about thirty, and I learned from the woman standing next to me that she was a doctor.

As I stood observing at the gate, I noticed about half of the 500 or more women arrested were probably under thirty, and the other half seemed to be over fifty. Very, very few – if any – were between thirty and fifty. I was told later that more than 200 women arrested were in their sixties and seventies. Approximately a thousand men were arrested, bringing our total number of resisters to more than 1,500 on this one day alone.

I stood for about three hours talking to a lot of women while waiting for all our resisters to be processed and moved into the holding areas. Many of them were from the San Diego area, representing several peace groups. They said more than two hundred of those arrested were from San Diego alone. Those women I spoke to represented groups such as Physicians for Social Responsibility; SANE/FREEZE; Beyond War; United Church of Christ; Catholic, Episcopal, Unitarian and Presbyterian Churches; and Seeds for Peace.

One of the detainees was Mary Pope. "Hi, my name is Lois and I heard you telling the lady next to you that you're from an Oceanside, CA, Catholic church. My eldest daughter, Debbie, lives in Oceanside with five of my grandchildren and they are Catholic. Which congregation are you involved with? I think Debbie would love to get involved. The only problem is that she is in her early thirties and very busy raising her children," I said.

"It is nice to meet you, Lois. My name is Mary Pope and I will be happy to contact your daughter when I return home. We are always looking for more people to join our group, and to learn the health hazards of nuclear testing. Even though she is busy raising her family it wouldn't hurt to come to our meetings and begin learning," Mary replied. "Let's exchange names and addresses. Here is my business card."

When the biggest part of the arresting was over, they started moving us into buses. By now I had removed my handcuffs. A woman physician had smuggled in a pair of scissors in her sock, so she cut the cuffs loose for many for us. They were made of a tough plastic, and cut our arms easily, so I already had black and blue marks after only three hours.

I was herded onto the first bus, the very first forty-six people to be bused on an hour's ride to Beatty, Nevada. While we were on the bus one of the arresting officers spent five minutes with each of us, filling out the forms for trespassing on government property. Of course, it wasn't really government property because the Shoshone Nation never accepted one penny for the land when it was taken from them. We were asked our names and addresses and naturally all of us gave false names and other information. In 1989 there weren't laptop computers with data bases to check personal information, so they had no way of checking who we were. The fine was $250 plus court costs. No one was to pay at this time. We were told they would send us a bill if they didn't decide to drop the charges. Obviously, they did drop the charges because none of us ever heard from them again.

While riding, I had a long conversation with the fifty-one-year-old woman sitting next to me. She was an Associate Professor of Sociology at San Diego University. She, too, was concerned for her children and grandchildren.

In Beatty, Nevada, we were taken to the local school and led into the gym. There, an officer explained the charges and then released us. We were informed that if they were going to follow through with the charges, we would hear from them. More government hot air, I guess, because how would they find us?

Bus after bus arrived for the next four hours until more than thirty buses had arrived and departed. The others from NJ were put on one of the last buses. Our support group arrived in the van about an hour after me and we all waited for the other members to finally join us.

I am now much more knowledgeable and more determined than ever to continue working to help end this dangerous nuclear era.

"He who passively accepts evil is as much involved as he who unjustly perpetrates it. He who accepts evil without protesting against it is really cooperating with it." –

Martin Luther King

Top: Our Princeton group entering the forbidden area. I got caught in the barbed wire fence, so they had to help me through! Bottom: Our Princeton group as we prepared to go into the forbidden area.

CHAPTER 3

MEETING OLZHAS SULEIMENOV

In December 1990, I volunteered for Parliamentarians for Global Action based in New York City. This organization works with parliament members throughout the world to introduce bills in their respective governments that bring about changes in laws concerning all types of peace issues. The hot issue in 1990 was to push for a nuclear moratorium to stop the five nuclear powers from testing nuclear weapons.

I helped organize a three-day meeting to be held in Washington D.C., advocating a nuclear testing moratorium. I invited my friend, Dolores, to accompany me and we drove down to D.C. to join the other committee members. After we checked into our hotel and unpacked our suitcases, we headed to the Parliamentarians field office. We hadn't been there very long when Aaron Tovish, the director of Parliamentarians, came rushing into the room.

"Could anyone possibly drive out to Dulles Airport to pick up the two British and Russian Parliament delegations that are arriving shortly? The driver assigned to pick them up is caught in traffic, and we need someone out there right now," he said.

"I'd be more than happy to drive to the airport, Aaron. Do you have access to a van? Dolores and I drove down in her compact car and there won't be room enough for everyone with their luggage."

"Yes, you can use the organization's van. Do you know how to get there?"

"Not exactly, but I have a good map and Dolores can direct me," I informed him as we jumped up to leave. Before we left, we made a large cardboard sign with the names "Olzhas Suleimenov" and "Vladimir Iakimets" on it in large black letters.

When we arrived at the International Arrivals gate, we worked our way through the crowd of people and stood in line next to all the limousine drivers waiting for their customers. We took turns holding the sign up high over our head so it could be easily seen. One flight after another arrived. Finally, after almost an hour of waiting, the passengers began arriving from the Aeroflot flight coming in from Moscow.

The waiting room soon vibrated with excitement as more than a hundred people gathered to greet their Soviet relatives or friends and the Russian language flowed throughout the room.

Most of those arriving had never been to the United States before because of the Cold War between our two nations. As the first passengers came through the arrivals revolving double door, we stood there witnessing families reuniting after many years apart. For most of them, this was a dream come true – to finally set foot on American soil. During the decades of Cold War between our two countries, no one was allowed entrance to America. Tears of joy flowed everywhere. As I looked around the room, almost every person was crying as they hugged their loved ones. It was such a powerful scene to witness that Dolores and I had tears in our eyes too. Only the limo drivers, who stood erect and motionless, seemed to be able to resist shedding tears. I just imagined they probably saw this scene every time they picked up a passenger arriving from the Soviet Union.

Finally, the double doors opened and a tall man with charcoal-black hair flowing as it touched his broad shoulders entered. He looked a lot like how I imagined a person from Mongolia would look, with striking slanted eyes and puffy cheeks. He walked with the demeanor of one who knew exactly who he was and what his mission in life entails. I knew immediately this was my Kazakh man who held the title of a People's Deputy in the Supreme Soviet of the Kremlin in Moscow. Soon, he saw our sign and recognized his name, and Dolores and I greeted him and his translator Vladimir.

The two British Parliament members arrived on their British Airways flight from Heathrow Airport in London, and we all headed back to the hotel where we were staying for the next few days. Along with Senator Tom Harkin of Iowa and Congressman Chris Smith of New Jersey, the group soon became known as the Tripartite Delegation of Parliament Members working on a moratorium to stop nuclear testing throughout the world.

When we arrived at the hotel, I informed our very important passengers they could freshen up and we would be at the front entrance at 6 pm to taxi them to a reception being held in their honor at the Hart Senate building. Dolores and I ran up to our room to put on our evening wear and makeup, stammering with enthusiasm.

At 6 pm our guests, freshly bathed and dressed in their handsome suits, met us in the lobby by the front entrance. This was the first trip to the United States for our Soviet guests, and they appeared as excited as we were. Dolores and I ushered them to the Hart Senate

Building. We arrived on the second floor to a crowded room of senators and congressmen. The atmosphere in the room vibrated with excitement! As we carried our glasses of Zinfandel, we made our way to the far wall where we could watch the senators and congressmen greeting Deputy Suleimenov and the other parliamentarians.

Our American politicians had extraordinarily little opportunity to meet and talk freely with a member of the Soviet Kremlin. Most of our legislators had never heard of Kazakhstan before they were invited to attend this evening reception. The affair was scheduled immediately following the end of the congressmen's workday, to ensure many could attend. Consequently, wives weren't invited, so Delores and I definitely felt privileged. We were in our glory.

"Dolores, this is one of the most thrilling evenings I can ever remember having," I exclaimed. "All my life, I was fascinated by the functioning of governments and the United Nations. I remember when I was fourteen, I wrote to the United Nations inquiring what I should do to qualify for a job someday. When I was seventeen, I ran for high school student council president. Standing here in this room in Washington D.C. with congressmen from not only the United States, but the Soviet Union and Great Britain is overwhelming to me," I told Dolores.

"Truthfully, I have been to more than a hundred cocktail parties in my life, but none of them were near as breathtaking as this. I'm so glad you invited me to come with you, Lois," my friend exclaimed.

We were just finishing our second glass of wine when I suddenly saw our handsome leader, six-foot-six tall Aaron Tovish, motioning with his finger over the top of everyone's heads for us to come to him. His bulging eyes seemed to be growing as large as golf balls and his mouth was twitching. I saw absolute horror on his face as we made our way over.

"Whatever is the matter, Aaron? You look like you just saw a ghost," I exclaimed.

"Lois, there is some terrible problem going on over there with Deputy Suleimenov. All he keeps telling me in his broken English is that we must help him," Aaron said. "Will you please go over there and do whatever is needed to help him with his problem?"

I looked over toward where Olzhas Suleimenov was standing and all I could see was a group of pitch-black-haired people in a huddle. I walked over to the circle of people surrounding Olzhas and asked his translator, Vladimir, what was wrong. Olzhas looked at me, assuming I carried some kind of authority, and quickly started explaining the situation in Russian. Vladimir began translating as fast as he could. As I listened and looked around the circle, the one phrase coming from all those around him was, "Please help us!"

The situation was pitiful. According to the Kazakh delegation, a thirty-four-year-old American man named Paul in California had arranged a peace walk with the Kazakh people that took place the past summer. The agreement was that one hundred Americans would go to Kazakhstan and spend twenty-five days as the guests of the Kazakh people. Paul took $2,000 from approximately eighty Americans each to allow them to participate on this trip. The other twenty were his personal friends who paid little or nothing. With that $160,000 he bought flight tickets and visas for the hundred American travelers, himself included. In 1990, a round-trip flight ticket to Kazakhstan, with a changeover in Moscow, was less than $700 on Pan Am airlines. That totaled about $70,000 for the flight and around $10,000 for the visas. The Kazakh organization had agreed to feed, transport and house the American guests free for the twenty-five days.

The Americans walked every day from one town or village to another throughout the outskirts of the capital, Almaty. They met, shook hands, and communicated with smiles, hugs and very limited Russian as they met thousands of Kazakh citizens along the road, often walking together. The Americans were treated like royalty for the entire twenty-five days. There were banquets every noon and evening, cultural events and speaking engagements everywhere. The American guests posed for thousands of pictures. They were invited into the people's homes and given their beds, while the local people graciously slept in their kitchens on the floor.

The remaining $80,000 of the money that Paul collected from the Americans was to be spent hosting the hundred Kazakh people who would come to America, starting with this group of twenty. Paul told the Kazakh organizers that he could not host a hundred at a time, so he insisted they had to send groups of twenty every couple of months. This group before me, seemingly distressed, was the first contingent of twenty visitors.

Olzhas helped the Kazakh peace organization purchase the twenty flight tickets and visas and made all their arrangements to come in the first fifteen days of December. This initial group comprised those who had donated substantially to host the Americans and make their visit to Kazakhstan the wonderful success it was. They were the business and professional people who made many financial sacrifices to make the peace walk in Kazakhstan happen.

About two weeks before they were to leave Kazakhstan for the United States, the man known as Paul called the Kazakh organization and said he couldn't host them until the next spring. When Olzhas was informed of this, he immediately telephoned Paul in California and told him in no uncertain terms that his twenty Kazakh people would be arriving in Washington D.C. on December 1, and Paul better see to it that they were well cared for.

I had never met Paul. He lived in California and this was the first I ever heard about him. When Vladimir interpreted what Paul had done to the people of Kazakhstan, I was horrified. Of course, I've heard of people pulling scams, but it was so hard to believe someone active in the peace movement would do such a thing. All I could think of was that someone had to undo the damage he had caused. Otherwise our peace movement would suffer a terrible blow when this hit the news.

Paul had already decided to be in Vietnam during the first two weeks of December to begin organizing a new peace walk there for the next summer. So, Paul called James, one of the young men whom he allowed to travel free on the trip to Kazakhstan and told him it was now his responsibility to host the twenty Kazakh people in D.C. James was twenty-two years old and didn't have a clue how to host them. He worked for the Washington D.C. soup kitchens and lived in a tiny two-room apartment.

On December 1, the twenty Kazakh business and professional people arrived at Dulles Airport in Washington D.C. James borrowed a van and made three trips that day, picking up seven people at a time. He had no idea where to house them, so he took them to the homeless shelters and housed them there. They ate in the D.C. soup kitchens. These were the wealthy professionals of Kazakhstan, wearing fur coats and visiting America for the first time. Imagine the shock, fear, and horror they went through those first five days in America! Olzhas arrived on December 5, and now all twenty of his kinsmen were here, outraged at how they were being treated.

"Lois, will you please help my people?" Olzhas asked me through his translator, his eyes pleading and hopeful. I was totally stunned. What could I do to help him and his people?

"I am so sorry, Mr. Suleimenov, but I'm not sure what I can do to help. I haven't any contacts here in Washington D.C. I live far away in Princeton, New Jersey," I told him.

"Dah! Dah! That would be wonderful if you take them to Princeton. My people have heard much about Princeton and I would be forever indebted to you, my friend Lois," Olzhas's translator reported as Olzhas extended his hand for me to shake.

"Well, okay, I'll do everything I can to take them up to Princeton, but I must go back home first to pick up a larger vehicle and make some arrangements for everyone. I will try to be back here by 5 pm tomorrow afternoon to pick them up," I said, while my mind was frantically calculating how I could possibly accomplish this.

Olzhas said this was a wonderful idea. He told his twenty comrades he would put them up in a D.C. hotel for the night, and I would return the next evening to take them to Princeton. Of course, they were all excited and enthusiastic at my promise, leaving me standing there in shock trying to figure out how I ever got myself into this predicament.

Dolores and I started back to our hotel room in silence. Finally, she quietly asked me, "Lois, how are we ever going to pull this off?"

"I don't know yet, Dolores. All I do know is that we must make it happen. Olzhas Suleimenov is one of the most influential people in the world right now. There are only three of the five nuclear powers even taking part in this Tripartite Delegation. China and France refused to participate, and the chance for a global moratorium on nuclear weapons is extremely important. Too important for us to fail when he looked into our eyes and asked us personally to help him. No matter how difficult this will be, we have been given a chance to help Olzhas Suleimenov and I am certain it will lead us to become actively involved on a much larger scale than we probably ever could imagine," I said.

When we entered our room, I ran to the phone and called Rose at her home in Ewing, New Jersey. Rose and Vladimir Herbeck were the eldest members of our growing little local group of peacemakers. Rose, a woman in her seventies, was born in Berlin, Germany, and Vladimir, in his eighties, was born in Moscow, Russia. They met in a Berlin underground bomb shelter during a heavy bombardment in the 1940s. They fell in love and were the first couple married in their Berlin neighborhood one week after the war ended. After immigrating to Canada, they eventually moved to Ewing, where they raised their children and remained the rest of their lives.

I told her the whole story and then asked, "Rose, will you please telephone Professor Falk, Professor Frank von Hippel, Professor Dietrich Fischer and everyone else you know to help find host families for twenty Soviets from Kazakhstan for the next eight nights? Tell them they can plan anything they want with their guests and find out how many guests they can each house. Please ask them to be in the Acme parking lot at the Princeton mall at 9 pm tomorrow evening to pick up their visitors. Okay?"

"From where? Kazakhstan? I don't even know where Kazakhstan is, and I'm from Germany. If I don't know where it is, I doubt if anyone else has ever heard of it either. Lois, what are you getting us into? How are you going to afford getting them all up here?" Rose asked.

"Somehow I'll find a way. Just please call as many of our friends as you must in order to get them all housed. Okay?"

"Okay. Dear God, I hope you know what you're doing," Rose said as she hung up.

Dolores and I were up at 5 am the next morning and on our way back to New Jersey. She dropped me off at my apartment and I told her I would rent a fifteen-passenger van and drive down to pick the group up. She asked if she should ride back with me, but we needed all the room to transport as many of their group as possible. I suggested that she help Rose find host families and explain to each host what had happened to them their first five days in our country. I went to the local Budget car rental service and rented a large van for a week, which was going to cost me a fortune on my income. I used a charge card and by noon, I was on my way back to D.C.

I arrived at their hotel a little before five that afternoon, and they were right there on the sidewalk waiting for me. We stuffed eighteen people and their luggage into the van, until there wasn't an inch of extra space left. With no translator to explain, I assumed the other two must have decided to remain in D.C. Big mistake! By 5:30 pm, we were on our way north and talk about an enthusiastic bunch of people! Even with the language barrier I could clearly understand they were a happy group of travelers, smiling and laughing as they pointed out the windows. Being so stuffed into the van never seemed to bother them at all. What I didn't know until eight months later, during my first trip into Kazakhstan, was what a really stuffed van or bus looked like. To them this was a piece of cake.

Now all I had to do for the next three-and-a-half hours while driving them safely to Princeton was hope and pray that Rose and Dolores had been successful in finding host families. Without a cell phone, I had no communication all day with my friends. Oddly enough, I didn't really worry about them finding homes. I just knew in my heart they would find all the help we needed. I was functioning totally on faith.

By 9 pm on any December night, it's usually pitch dark in Princeton, so I was very surprised when I saw so much light as we approached the Acme parking lot. That is when I had the most wonderful surprise waiting for me. At the back of the parking lot was a huge semi-circle with ten cars lined up, all sitting there with their headlights on waiting to meet the first Soviet Kazakhs to ever visit Princeton. Each of the nine families took two guests. Professor von Hippel came up and invited Dolores and me to join his guests at his home for a late supper he and his wife had prepared. I thanked him and he ran off to join his new friends.

I turned to Dolores, who had helped me assign everyone to each of the families, and she and I started laughing. "I can't believe we did it, Dolores. Will you go over to Frank von Hippel's home with me for supper?" I asked my friend.

"I wouldn't miss it for the world," she said. We agreed to meet at my apartment in twenty minutes.

As Dolores arrived, my telephone rang. I answered it, but at first, I could not clearly understand the person on the other end of the line. However, with a good deal of effort I finally figured out the caller was one of the two Kazakhs I had left in D.C. They had come up on the train and were at the Princeton station. I told them we would be there in ten minutes to pick them up.

"Dolores, what are we going to do with these two? Wait a minute, if you will allow me to come over to your apartment and sleep in your guestroom, they can have my apartment here. What do you think?" I asked her.

"That sounds like a good idea to me. Since we haven't more host families, and we're both working all week, that is probably the best solution. We'll ask each host family if these two can spend one day and evening with them, along with their other two guests," Dolores said with a smile on her face.

Ten minutes later, we found our lost Kazakhs waiting on the Princeton train station platform, luggage in hand. We took them with us to Frank von Hippel's home where Frank and Barbara had a spread laid out that was fit for a king. It was a glorious evening, and after each toast, our new Kazakh friends came up and hugged us over and over again. They couldn't hide their exuberance. They sang their Soviet songs while we hummed along with them and they joyfully danced until they flopped from exhaustion.

At the end of the evening, we brought our two new arrivals to my apartment. Dolores came up to help me pack my suitcase and carry it to her car. Then I began to show the two guests the refrigerator and indicate other necessities they might need to be comfortable.

"Oh, nyet, nyet! You here. Sergei go with friend," Yuri said as he tried to take my suitcase out of my hand.

"Oh, nyet, nyet! I go with Dolores. You and Sergei will stay here in my apartment," I said as I pulled frantically on my suitcase. Dolores and I practically ran out my apartment door and down the stairs, with both our guests yelling for us to stay.

Once we were in Dolores' apartment, we each slumped into a chair and I thought we'd never stop laughing. The funny part of it all is, they were both about our ages – we were both single – and they were really good looking. But I knew from having previously walked the Soviet–American Peace Walk in 1988, and my visit to Volgograd in 1989, that no Soviet could get a visa to come to America unless they were leaving a spouse back home. And that was not acceptable!

The last day of their visit, I picked up fifteen of them, and the other five took the train back to D.C. I took my loaded van of visitors into New York City and we spent the day touring and shopping. That evening, we walked around the Christmas Tree at Rockefeller Center before departing for our four-hour drive to Washington. We arrived in the middle of the night to the hotel where Olzhas had arranged for them to stay on their last night in the USA, and I shared a room with two of the ladies. Early next morning, we packed the van and headed out to Dulles Airport with half the group. I dropped the first ten people off and went back for the other ten. That afternoon, I stood in the airport at the entrance to their flight and hugged every one of them as they boarded their plane to go back to Kazakhstan. In those last nine days, my friends had undone all the damage that Paul in California had forced on them, and they went home a very happy group of people. One of the women, Umyt Sakarieva, became a very good friend. She arranged the four future trips that I made into Kazakhstan. Three years later, she returned to America for a life-saving surgery at the Pennsylvania University Hospital in Philadelphia. But that is another story to come!

To this day, Umyt jokes about those first five days in Washington D.C., and says it was a real eye-opener for all her delegation. They ended up witnessing both extremes of our American society.

<u>Top:</u> Olzhas Suleimenov with WCD members (from left in front row) Jean Dorgan, Dolores Hewitt, Olzhas and me. <u>Bottom:</u> Bob Moore enjoying the Kazakh delegation at the home of Professor Frank von Hippel in Princeton.

Members of the Kazakh Delegation enjoying Professor Frank von Hippel's welcoming dinner at his home in Princeton

CHAPTER 4

KICK-OFF FOR U.N. PARTIAL TEST BAN TREATY (PTBT)

Soon after we bid goodbye to our new Kazakh friends, I received a telephone call from Aaron Tovish at the Parliamentarians for Global Action home office in New York City. He had another project that needed volunteers and wanted to know if we were interested in helping him again. Nothing could have pleased Dolores and me more than to jump on the Jersey Transit train at Princeton Junction and head back into Manhattan for another round of excitement. And these next couple of weeks turned into a real whirlwind of unexpected surprises.

Because I was now becoming so actively involved with my volunteer work, I had set up a thriving commercial and residential cleaning service in the Princeton area, and my son Michael was managing it with me. Therefore, it worked out perfectly to have him run the business as the head supervisor over our employees while I trekked off to New York City.

Dolores and I spent every minute possible at the Parliamentarians office, helping to organize a big celebration to be held the night before the Partial Test Ban Treaty Amendment Conference opened at the United Nations.

"Dolores, I never dreamed I would ever have the opportunity to organize a black tie champagne reception and dinner in the Tower Suite of the Time & Life Building on the Avenue of the Americas in New York City," I said as I licked stamps on our invitation envelopes.

"I can't believe all the featured speakers and dignitaries who are attending. Not only is Deputy Olzhas Suleimenov representing the Kremlin in Moscow, but Senator Tom Harkin is representing the USA and Allan Rogers, the MP from the United Kingdom, makes three nuclear nations that will be in attendance," Dolores said.

"Yes, and the Honorable Warren Allmand, MP from Canada, is to give the welcoming remarks. Dr. Olafur Grimsson, the Minister of Finance in Iceland will be giving the concluding remarks," I added. "Remember Mr. Ali Alatas, the Foreign Minister of Indonesia, whom we met a few weeks ago in Washington D.C.? He's giving the key-note address."

We invited all the UN delegates and our World Citizen Diplomat members, and twelve of our members were able to attend, including my daughter Patty and her husband Townsend.

Since both of us would be not only attending but also escorting many dignitaries during the next few weeks, Dolores and I quickly realized we had to do a lot of research pertaining to the PTBT. The minute we found our seats on the Princeton to New York train at 7 am, each morning, we pulled out our notes and started cramming for the biggest test of our lives – the global nuclear testing history and why the tests needed to be stopped.

In December 1990, approximately only one in a hundred American households owned any kind of personal computer. I was still using a computer at Kinko's office supply store, and nothing like Google or Wikipedia even existed then. Therefore, all research pertaining to the PTBT had to be done at the local library.

"Dolores, I spent a few hours last night at the library and finally found some background on the PTBT. Here is what I learned so far," I said. "The concept of banning nuclear testing originated with arms control advocates in the early 1950s, after the United States conducted more than fifty nuclear explosions between 1945 and 1953. In 1954, Prime Minister Nehru of India proposed the elimination of all nuclear test explosions worldwide, but no treaty was launched as a result of public concern in the context of the Cold War. Thus, nuclear tests resumed, but in 1961, Physicians for Social Responsibility documented the presence of strontium-90 (a by-product of nuclear tests) in the teeth of children around the world – confirming that nuclear tests pose serious public health dangers."

I went on to explain to Dolores that in 1963, a Partial Test Ban Treaty (PTBT) was adopted banning tests in the atmosphere, under water, or in space. Then in 1988 – the twenty-fifth anniversary of the signing of the PTBT – an amendment proposal was submitted. Now, January 8–18, 1991, the UN is holding the 4th Review Amendment Conference. This is a very crucial time for the resumption of negotiations toward attaining a CTBT in the near future. The outcome of this conference is to encourage a CTBT before 1996! Then all countries throughout the world must ratify this treaty within twenty years to make it a permanent global law.

The evening we have been working on is the celebration of the opening of the test ban treaty conference entitled "Passing the Torch." We scheduled it for Sunday evening, January 6, 1991, the night before the UN conference was to begin.

At 6:30 pm, the Champagne Reception formally opened the evening activities. It was breathtaking for Dolores and me to greet each attendee. Dolores, Aaron and I took turns escorting each group as they arrived in the Tower Suite and we introduced them among all those who were already in attendance.

Many reporters were interviewing, and pictures were being taken throughout the room.

The dinner itself began at 7:30 pm sharp, opened by Honorable Warren Allmand, MP from Canada, with his welcoming remarks.

Celebration of the Opening of the
Test Ban Treaty Conference

"Passing the Torch"

6 January 1990, 6:30 to 10:00 p.m.
Tower Suite, Time & Life Building, 50th St. and 6th Ave., New York

6:30 Champagne Reception

7:30 Black-Tie Dinner

Welcoming Remarks: Hon. Warren Allmand, MP, Canada

The Tripartite Delegation
Sen. Tom Harkin, US
Mr. Allan Rogers, MP, UK
Mr. Olzhas Suleimenov, Deputy, USSR

Main Course

Keynote Address: H.E. **Mr. Ali Alatas, Foreign Minister, Indonesia**

Concluding Remarks: H.E. Dr. Ólafur Grímsson, Minister of Finance, Iceland

Top: I am with Aaron Tovish, Director of Parliamentarians for Global Action, at the Celebration Opening of the Nuclear Test Ban Treaty Conference at the UN. Bottom: Aaron Tovish, Olzhas Suleimenov and his translater, Vladimir Iakamits at a planning session in New Jersey

TOP: Jan. 6, 1991—Dolores, Pakistani Senator Jived Jabar, and Lois at the ballroom dance for the UN Test Ban Treaty Conference in NYC.
BOTTOM: Iowa Senator Tom Harkin, Peoples Deputy of the Supreme Soviet Honorable Olzhas Suleimenov, and Turkish journalist.

**The Citizens Movement preparing for the Opening of the
Nuclear Test Ban Treaty Conference in NYC, being led by Olzhas
Suleimenov, Deputy of the Supreme Soviet in USSR**

Kick-off for UN Partial Test Ban Treaty (PTBT)

Jan. 6, 1991 – U.N., NYC Nuclear Test Ban Treaty Conference. Dolores Hewitt, WCD member and Iowa Senator Tom Harkin.

Jan. 6, 1991 – At U.N. Nuclear Test Ban Treaty Conference in NYC. Dolores and I with Honorable Olzhas Suleimenov, Soviet Deputy, USSR; his translater Vladimir Iakimets; and Dr. and Mrs. Olafur Grimsson, Minister of Finance, Iceland.

Jan. 6, 1991 – U.N. Nuclear Test Ban Conference sponsored by Parliamentarians for Global Action in NYC. Dolores and me with Allan Rogers, MP from the UK and another guest.

Dolores enjoying dinner with other guests of the evening.

Dolores enjoying lunch with the Senators at the Senate Hart Building in Washington DC.

CHAPTER 5

CLOSING A SOVIET TEST SITE

In the spring of 1991 my new friend, Olzhas Suleimenov, returned to the United States as a guest of the Philadelphia Poetry Society. Besides serving in the Kremlin as a People's Deputy of the Supreme Soviet representing the Republic of Kazakhstan, Olzhas was the most famous Kazakh poet alive.

After his commitment in Philadelphia, I picked him up with his translator, Vladimir Iakimets, in my minivan and we spent a week touring the eastern United States from Boston to Washington D.C. In Massachusetts, we spent a day with Dr. Bernard Lown, Olzhas' friend and cardiologist. Dr. Lown was the recipient of the Nobel Peace Prize in 1985 for his part as cofounder of the International Physicians for the Prevention of Nuclear War (IPPNW) in 1980.

In Washington D.C., we spent two days with Senator Tom Harkin and several Senate colleagues who were working with Olzhas on a moratorium to end nuclear testing globally.

The night before I drove Olzhas to JFK, we had an exciting, elegant potluck dinner in his honor at the home of Jim and Gail Firestone on Carnegie Lake in Princeton. We refer to it as an "elegant potluck" because we wore our most beautiful cocktail or Sunday dresses – many sparkling in colorful sequins – and brought our favorite covered dish to share. The dinner was a wonderful success. After the meal, approximately eighty of us congregated in the living room. Jim and Gail were the owners of Firestone Realty, a successful real estate company located in the center of Princeton. They joined our growing little peace organization and offered their help whenever needed. They lived in a lovely home which had a magnificently large living room, large enough to accommodate our extensive crowd for Olzhas to speak to. We brought all the couches and chairs from the library and dining room into the living room once dinner was over. Soon, we had filled every couch and chair and the youngest in attendance sat on the floor and windowsills.

For more than two hours, we listened to Olzhas describe through his translator what it was like to be a People's Deputy in the Supreme Soviet and what life was like in Kazakhstan.

"Tonight is a dream come true for me," Olzhas exclaimed as soon as we all found a place to sit. He looked so handsome with his soft, shiny black hair flowing over his right eye and covering his ears. He certainly didn't look fifty-four years old to me. He was wearing his dark gray suit and red tie, the same ones I remembered him wearing last December when I took him to the Hart Senate Building in Washington D.C. to meet with Senator Tom Harkin and more than a hundred senators and congressmen.

As I looked at him standing there in front of us, I figured he must be about 5'11", although to me he resembled a giant. It's interesting how someone appears to you once you realize how intelligent and worldly they are.

Olzhas continued, "As I look around this room, I see the America I always envisioned. There are young and old alike; every skin tone imaginable; and having met each of you during dinner I know you represent many countries. You are the true melting pot of the world."

We were all spellbound. As I looked around the room, I saw every eye focused on him and every head stretching to hear what he had to say. He told us how communism was crumbling and how things were already getting exceedingly difficult in his country. I could not believe all the questions my friends were bombarding him with, but both Olzhas and his translator seemed to enjoy every moment of it.

Finally, Rose Herbeck said, "Olzhas, we would like to help you in some way. What can we do to help you and your people as you move through this very difficult time?"

Olzhas' response was instant. "More than anything else, we need medicines. We have none. Not even aspirin to relieve the pain for the children suffering from leukemia. If you could send us medicine, that would help us so much and we would be forever grateful."

That evening we took up a collection and early the next morning, I went to CVS on Nassau Street and purchased $500 worth of medicines. I bought children's Tylenol, baby aspirin, Pepto Bismol, and antibiotic salves. I filled my small carry-on suitcase with the medicines and drove to pick up Olzhas and Vladimir to take them to the airport. As we drove the Belt Parkway, I remember saying to him, "Olzhas, I'm almost embarrassed to send you back with this small suitcase of medicines. What good will this tiny amount of medicines do for even a small part of your country? It will barely help on just one floor of only one hospital throughout your whole nation."

Olzhas' response was immediate: "Lois, you have no idea what these medicines are going to do. I will arrive home in two days, and reporters will greet us at the airport in Almaty. I will tell the people of my country about my trip to America. I will tell them how you spent a week driving me all over the east coast so I could try to find help as we move into this difficult period. I'll tell them how your friends asked what they could do to help, and when I told them we need medicines for our children, they immediately sent medicines back with me. It isn't important how much was sent. The important thing is that American people do care about us and are reaching out to help in our time of need.

"For more than half a century, our two countries have been locked in a cold war. In our schools, we were taught from childhood to fear the Americans because they were greedy and powerful war mongers. We were never told the whole truth about the attack on Pearl Harbor, and when the atomic bombs exploded in Japan, our government said, 'See, we told you how evil the Americans are.' My people grew to fear the Americans and their democracy.

"Now our communist system is in shambles and we will soon have to decide what direction to go in as a nation. I have been to the USA twice now, and I know how good the American people are, and that democracy is definitely the way for us to go. I want you, Lois, to bring groups of Americans to Kazakhstan so my people can meet you and hear you speak. This will help them begin to trust American people, and they won't be quite so afraid of democracy. Will you please bring a group of people soon?"

I promised Olzhas I would put a delegation together immediately. As soon as I returned to Princeton, I drove straight to my friend Dolores' home and told her about Olzhas' invitation. We immediately mapped out our plans and began calling all the members of our growing peace organization.

It cost each of us $650 for the round-trip flight from JFK to Moscow on Pan Am and from Moscow to Almaty, Kazakhstan, on Aeroflot. I drove to Washington D.C. with everyone's passports to request our visas, which cost another $150 each. Because the important invitation came from the Kremlin, our government issued visas for my group the same day I applied for them. Our entourage consisted of myself, my best friend, Doloris, another close friend, Fran, and four other members of our growing peace organization.

The seven of us arrived in Moscow just two weeks after Boris Yeltzin stood on the tank in front of the Kremlin White House and faced down an attempted coup by the communist party opposed to Premier Mikhail Gorbachev and the breakup of the USSR. It was a time when democracy was sprouting up everywhere. We walked Red Square where people with bullhorns were proclaiming a new life in Russia. "Glasnost" and "Perestroika" rang out from every corner. Olzhas and all the other People Deputies of the crumbling Soviet Union were on one side of the Kremlin Wall, trying to save the old USSR while we seven Americans were on the other side of the wall joining all the Soviet citizens feverishly clamoring for democracy. What a historic time to be in Russia!

After three days in Moscow, we flew to Almaty, Kazakhstan. Umyt and her husband, Zhamil, greeted us with about a dozen others as we disembarked from our Aeroflot plane at midnight on a pitch-black runway. Umyt had met Dolores and me in December of 1990 when she accompanied the group of twenty Kazakh citizens on their first trip to the United States and we rescued the group from a very bad situation. We were all very excited to see each other again.

When we entered the airport, we were shocked to see a long banquet table in the middle of the terminal laden with food platters, drinks and exotic, colorful flowers. Overhead were the most dazzling, impressive chandeliers I had ever seen. We marveled at the elegance and fine foods and wondered if this was just a taste of things to come for us in this alien country.

We spent the next four hours eating their exquisite food and enjoying every imaginable Kazakh alcoholic fruit drink, all accompanied with continuous toasts to our friendship and the future between our two distant countries.

Escorted by our new Kazakh friends, we boarded another Aeroflot airplane and flew to Pavlodar, a region in north eastern Kazakhstan situated along the Irtysh River on the southern edge of the west Siberian plain. After a brief rest, we boarded the lead bus with twelve other buses following us, heading toward the border of the Semipalatinsk test site. This three-hour ride on the poorly paved roads took us past some of the famous flat steppes of Kazakhstan, which turn into semi-desert in the southwest. Soon, we saw local Kazakh citizens sitting in front of their yurts. Kazakhstan is a nation of black-haired people with olive shaped eyes, looking a lot like Mongolian people I had seen in photographs. They smiled and waved as we passed by. I was overwhelmed with a mixed feeling of awe and excitement to experience such an adventure.

I shall never forget our arrival! The scene through the windows of our bus was unforgettable: about 7,000 Kazakh nomads had gathered in the noon-day desert sun – waiting to celebrate the closing of their nuclear test site with the first Americans they had ever seen. We disembarked and spent several hours standing on a huge stage they built in the desert, listening to speeches and songs. From four gigantic six-foot-high speakers, two on each side of the stage, the music floated out into the desert like the breeze along the sea. The exotic music sounded exhilarating – very different from any music I had ever heard. In the distance, at the perimeter of the celebration, we could see a large yurt, a round Kazakh tent that the local nomadic herders lived in as they moved around on the steppes of Kazakhstan with their sheep.

"Lois, the mayor of Semipalatinsk would like to invite you and your American friends to join him and the local organizers of this celebration to partake of our national Kazakh meal. Everything is ready in the yurt up ahead," Umyt said through her husband's translation.

We had just finished participating in the ribbon-hanging ceremony, where everyone tied a brightly colored ribbon on the limb of a tree planted in the desert sand to represent those they knew who died of radiation poisoning caused by the nuclear testing.

The yurt was white and decorated with colorful blue embroidery on the outside. On the inside, white lace curtains surrounded the top half and orange walls around the lower half revealed white designs. The mayor directed us to sit Indian style on the carpeted floor, scattering us among the Kazakh dignitaries he included. Altogether, there were fourteen of us. The mayor sat directly across from me and his young female translator sat to my left. They brought all the food in from outside the yurt.

"Thank you very much for inviting us to this lovely dinner, Mayor Kuiden," I said. The mayor appeared to be only in his late thirties; he was good looking with a winning smile. To me, he possessed all the characteristics of an aspiring modern-day politician – handsome, beaming, and attentive; I felt like I was the most important person in the world.

"Lois, we are honored with your presence today and very proud to share our national meal with the first Americans to ever walk among us. My translator, Aiga, will explain each of our foods along with the traditions behind them," the mayor explained.

Aiga began by explaining the first of many customs. "Whenever a guest is welcomed by a Kazakh host into a shepherd's yurt to enjoy their national meal, the guest is first offered a piala (a small bowl) with tea. Another piala will be passed around with flat, round bread, dried fruits, nuts, sweets, and cream kaymak butter (sour cream), which is made from the traditional sheep milk."

I noticed several men as we entered the yurt attending an open fire where they were cooking a young lamb on a spit. They also had liquid boiling in a pot and when ready, they brought a boiled sheep's head into the yurt on a brightly painted ceramic platter and placed it in front of me. I was truly shocked, and my traveling companions gasped in disbelief. The head looked remarkably real, and fully intact. Because it had been boiled, it had no discoloration.

Aiga continued, "This is the koy-bas, the boiled sheep head. It is always placed before the most honored guest. First, you are to cut off the two ears and give the first one to your best friend and then the second one to a new friend."

It was at this moment that I began to realize what a privilege it was for us to be representing the America these warm, friendly people knew very little about and had never visited. We were their most honored guests! From this moment on, the rest of the day floated by as if I were living in a dream.

"Oh dear, I hope this knife is sharp enough to cut them off," I said as I attempted to cut the first ear off. Surprisingly enough, it came off easily and I put it on a dish and passed it to Dolores. She and I had been friends since I first arrived in Princeton back in 1987.

Then I cut off the second ear and presented it to my new friend Zhamil.

Aiga continued. "Next, you are to scoop all the loose parts and liquid from the head into a bowl." This made me quite squeamish, and fortunately the mayor came to my rescue. He leaned over and scooped everything from the skull into a big bowl, which was mostly the brain, and then passed me the bowl and spoon as he asked me to take a taste. I opened my mouth in shock! He wanted me to eat this white mushy substance. But as I scanned the circle of participants, all eyes focused on me. I looked into the bowl, up at the mayor, and then back into the bowl. I gathered all the courage in my body and took a taste. When I did this, all the local Kazakhs in our yurt clapped and smiled. This was an honor to them, and as little as I knew about protocol, I knew it was important to partake of their national meal. The rest of the meal – the salads, vegetable dishes, and lamb – were delicious. Traditionally, Kazakh cuisine consists of many meat dishes featuring horse meat, mutton and occasionally a young lamb. The cooking techniques and major ingredients have been strongly influenced by the nation's nomadic way of life. We were served one of such dishes, which was very tasty.

But no feast would be complete without a celebratory drink. From large pitchers they poured us a special brew, and everyone stood up to make a toast. Having already downed at least six vodka and alcoholic fruit beverages earlier, I was accustomed to standing for toasts! But when I took a sip I almost gagged. It tasted to me like liquid chalk mixed with a thimble of scotch and a big squirt of Worcestershire sauce. It was horrible!

I asked Aiga, "What is this unusual drink? I don't think I've tasted anything quite like it."

"This is the national drink of Kazakhstan," Aiga said. "It is called kumis. It is fermented for 78 to 120 hours."

"Oh, I understand. It is similar to how we ferment beer or wine," I said.

"No, Lois. This does not come from grapes or hops or barley. This is horse milk! Fermented horse milk. It is made from fresh mare's milk fermented in big skin bags. The alcohol content in kumis is created by the root of aconite, which is added to leaven it."

All my American friends heard her description and every face turned bright red with astonishment.

But our hosts assured us, "The more you drink it, the more you grow to like it!"

Neither my American companions nor I took another sip of kumis, but it didn't matter. Somehow, we passed all their tests, and after enjoying their meal and lots of toasts we ended the evening by dancing in the desert sand as the sun fell behind the horizon.

Out of this experience grew the creation of World Citizen Diplomats. The seven of us who spent these three weeks in Kazakhstan came back to the USA determined to erase the fear and stereotyping that had been flourishing for more than half a century between the USSR and the USA. We called every person we knew and began meeting at the Woodrow Wilson School at Princeton University once a week to construct the by-laws and statement of purpose for our new organization. We applied for and received our 501(c)(3) in 1992, declaring us an NGO (nongovernmental organization).

From 1992 through 1995, we made six more trips into Kazakhstan, Kyrgyzstan, Uzbekistan, and Russia, building dialogue with the people of a remote and foreign land. We also created the Peace 2000 Caravan, and now international delegations of men and women from many nations are traveling around the world to build dialogue and break down stereotypes and misconceptions people have of one another.

One of the people who traveled with us as a citizen diplomat was Yuri Kuidin of Kazakhstan, a professional photographer who uses his camera to educate people about the deadly legacy of nuclear testing. The following story is of how the Kazakh people managed to close the Semipalatinsk test site in 1990. It is a true example of "People Power" – in the ailing Soviet Union. How I wish I could have been there in February 1989, when the people made their choice to stand up against the nuclear testing. But at least I was there in September 1991, when Kazakh President Nazarbayev formally announced the closing. Here is the story of how these courageous people forced the government to close their nuclear testing site.

Kazakhstan was the second largest republic of the former Soviet Union, a state of mainly nomadic people who traveled with their sheep along the vast steppes of this central Asian nation located to the south of Russia. The former Soviet Union had chosen the enormous and sparsely inhabited territories of the Kazakh people as testing ground. Here, during the forty years from 1949 to 1989, the Soviet Union performed more than 400 nuclear tests spread all over the country, first above ground, then underground. Even the underground tests vented lots of radiation into the air.

Almost everyone on earth has heard about the Chernobyl nuclear accident and the terrible radiation problems experienced by people in the Ukraine and Belarus. It poisoned the air and land and killed or ruined the health of millions of people. The problems will continue to haunt the citizens of that region for many years.

In Kazakhstan, testing was conducted over a forty-year period, and only very slowly the genocidal nature of these nuclear tests began to dawn on the citizens of the Semipalatinsk Region. As the years passed, the people there began to witness changes in their health. Birth defects, leukemia, other forms of cancer, and many new diseases never heard of before began to appear and increase rapidly.

Olzhas Suleimenov, representing his home republic of Kazakhstan, started to witness the suffering of the people. He became more and more concerned as he saw an increasing rate of cancer. He informed his colleagues in the Supreme Soviet at the Kremlin that the nuclear testing resulted in serious health problems in his region. No one paid any attention to him. The region was far away from the Kremlin in Moscow and very few of the people deputies had any knowledge of radiation diseases. Out of sight – out of mind!

In February 1989, as a direct result of two underground tests at the Semipalatinsk test site, clouds containing huge amounts of radioactive gases passed over the inhabited areas. A military pilot at a base not far from the test site informed Olzhas that all the dosimeters in the town showed very high levels of radiation. These dosimeters had been installed in the kindergartens and schools for the children of the military officers, and the pilot was very concerned about the future health of his children. All criticism and questions regarding the tests were strictly taboo and the citizens were afraid to talk because it could lead to arrest by the secret police. Olzhas, nevertheless, decided to make an appeal to his people, and the opportunity came later in the month when he was invited to appear on TV to speak about the culture of Kazakhstan and to read his poetry.

Speaking in a direct transmission on national Kazakh television, Olzhas laid his prepared speech aside and, looking straight into the camera, told his people that it was time for them to rise up and speak out against the terrible crime that was being committed on them and their land. "The tests are not harmless as we have all been told for many years," he said. "The cold war is over. Why should we continue testing when there is no longer an enemy?" He said the best way for the Soviet Union to prove to the world that the cold war was indeed over was to stop testing and start reductions of the nuclear arsenals. Olzhas told the viewers that American peace activists were pushing to close their Nevada test site, and the people of Kazakhstan should start the process. "If we close our test site, then Nevada and others would stop also," he said. "No one in the Kremlin will pay attention to me about our serious situation here, so it is up to you citizens to do something." In conclusion, he invited the viewers to come to his office at the Union Writers Guild the next day at 10 am and promised to help them organize a people's movement against the nuclear tests.

The next day, a freezing cold one, February 28, 1989, Olzhas soon found his office a bit on the small side. More than 5,000 people showed up, so they had to stand outside the building with Olzhas speaking from a second-floor balcony. That day, they organized a peoples' movement and named it the "Nevada–Semipalatinsk Anti-nuclear Movement" to connect with the nuclear resisters in the USA. Olzhas wrote an appeal to the government of the USSR and during the first few weeks, over two million citizens of Kazakhstan signed this appeal. Peaceful demonstrations by ordinary citizens were held in the streets of cities, towns, and villages throughout Kazakhstan. Soon, there were thousands of people peacefully protesting the nuclear genocide.

As a result of these actions of protest, eleven of the eighteen tests planned for that year were stopped.

After the next explosion on October 19, 1989, 130,000 Kazakh miners declared they would go on an unlimited strike if the tests continued. Olzhas came out in the Supreme Soviet session with a decisive demand to close the nuclear testing site. In November, the Supreme Soviet adopted a resolution binding the government to discuss the issue to close the Semipalatinsk test site. Less than eight months after the formation of the anti-nuclear movement, President Gorbachev announced the first moratorium, ending the Soviet nuclear testing. It became the world's first test site to be permanently closed by democratic discussion and decision. In August 1991, President Nazarbayev made a formal statement that no one would ever test another weapon in the territory of Kazakhstan, a true triumph for the citizens of the country.

We arrived in their country soon after this announcement by President Nazarbayev and witnessed the closing of this site. The Kazakh people set a courageous example for the whole world to see and follow. They had dared to speak out and march in the streets even when the communist system was still in place. They didn't throw stones, or break windows, or raid stores, or rape women and children, or kill anyone. They just peacefully demonstrated until the testing site was closed.

Olzhas Suleimenov (center) Kazakh poet, Peoples Deputy in the Supreme Soviet of the Kremlin, and leader/organizer of the peoples campaign to close the nuclear test site after 40 years of testing.

Thousands of citizens of Kazakhstan went into the streets in protest of the nuclear tests in Semipalatinsk

Top:: I was presented flowers by an adorable little Kazakh girl in Pavlodar, Bottom: We danced to beautiful exotic music!

Approximately 7,000 Kazakh nomads celebrating
the closing of the Soviet nuclear test site and
enjoying the speeches of the first Americans they
ever met.

I had the privilege to speak to thousands of Kazakh citizens, bringing a message of peace and hope from the American people.

Speaking to approximately 7,000 Kazakh nomads, all participating in the final closing of the Soviet nuclear test site in Semipalatinsk.

Our group of seven Americans standing on the stage with Kazakh dignitaries.

Top: A lovely Kazakh lady wearing her native attire. Bottom: Kazakh and American citizens celebrating

A group picture of American and Kazakh citizens in front of the yurt where we enjoyed their National Meal.

The Kazakh people made me feel welcome and proud to represent my country as an American Citizen Diplomat.

Mission accomplished
Local delegation plants seeds for 'citizen diplomacy'

By Cathy Anderson
Staff Writer

Most of the 1,000 Kazakhs who greeted their van outside the closed nuclear test site had never seen an American citizen before. Hundreds of them jockeyed for position, vying for the opportunity to touch the "American-ns" just once.

Camill Harris of Kingston was one of the six members of the World Citizens Movement to take a three-week trek across the Soviet Union just one week after the failed Soviet coup d'etat. She recalls the highlight of the trip — the celebration at Semipalatinsk — that changed her life.

"We got off the van at Semipalatinsk, and people swarmed around us. One little girl followed me, kissing my back. If I moved from one circle, and was alone very briefly, another swarm of people would encircle me. They were so filled with love for us. It really has changed my life because I felt love from people I didn't even know.

"It really cracked a shell. I don't think I'll ever be the same. I appreciate America more because we have more conveniences, but I am so thankful for that opportunity."

The World Citizens Movement, formerly the Soviet-American Relations Committee, is headquartered on Witherspoon Street. Of the approximately 75 New Jersey members, mostly from the Princeton area, six made the Soviet Union tour Aug. 27 to Sept. 14.

The small but ardent group left just one week after the failed coup d'etat. At the advice of the U.S. State Department, the group canceled its trip Aug. 19, only to reschedule it three days later when President Mikhail Gorbachev regained power.

The six movement members plunked down $1,500 each and hopped a plane to Prague. Three weeks later, they said, they headed back to the States, mission accomplished — they planted the seeds for worldwide citizen diplomacy.

The itinerary: Prague, Moscow, Volgograd, Alma Ata, Pavladar, Kazakhstan, Issek Kool and Kergesia.

It was the celebration at Semipalatinsk, where they were honored with the ritual of the national meal, that meant the most to the movement members.

"We (World Citizens Movement) have been actively involved in nuclear disarmament for the past four years," explained Lois A. Nicolai, chairwoman of the movement and executive director of the New Jersey chapter of Peace Child.

In a speech to almost 8,000 Kazakhs outside Semipalatinsk, Ms. Nicolai said she was proud to represent the American people at such a historic celebration. "I said that we were so proud of these people because they've made an example for the world. I told them we hoped that, with their help and the rest of the world's help, we could close the other four test sites."

"I felt a lot of love," added Ms. Harris. "I stood there with tears coming down because I had never been treated like that before. I felt like I was in a movie, a Ghandi movie."

Frances Marasco of Trenton said she was impressed with the Russian people. "They were very solicitous and very warm. I felt as though I could physically touch them because they were such wonderful and warm people. That surprised me because all my life we were taught to be afraid of Russia."

What really touched Ms. Marasco was the respect the Russian people held for Americans. "There were times when they were asked to remain seated in the planes so the Americans could leave first. That sort of hurt me, to think that we were treated differently. They said not to worry about that. Russians are used to taking orders."

Dolores Hewitt of Princeton said, "It makes you more aware of the common humanity in all of us. We seem so much alike. We have the same kind of sense of humor. They poke fun at themselves all the time. We seemed to hit it right off."

An upshot of the trip was the promise of more exchanges to come, potentially 12 in the next year.

"It's all about citizen diplomacy. I know that now," said Ms. Nicolai. "The whole world really needs that because it's an opportunity for people of different countries of the world to get to know each other, to relate to each other as people, not as politicians."

CHAPTER 6 – PART 1

EDUCATING THE AMERICAN PEOPLE ON THE "HORRORS OF THE MUSHROOM"

Ring – Ring – Ring –

"Hello!" I yelled into the mouthpiece after running to catch the telephone call.

"Hello. Please may I speak with Mrs. Lois Nicolai?" the woman's voice responded.

"Yes, this is Lois Nicolai. May I help you?"

"This is the Kremlin operator calling for Professor Vladimir Iakimets here in Moscow. One moment please," she said, as her voice disappeared into a bunch of static. A few moments later, I heard the familiar voice of Olzhas Suleimenov's translator in Russia.

"Hello, my friend Lois, this is Vladimir. How are you? Olzhas and I send our good wishes to you."

"I am wonderful, Vladimir. What a nice surprise to hear from you. I hope you are both in good health this cold winter."

"Yes, we are both fine. I must make call short, so I come right to important matter. We were contacted by David Brown in California that there is very big three-day nuclear moratorium event coming up at American test site in Los Vegas this April. Are you going?" Vladimir inquired.

"Truthfully, Vladimir, I hadn't heard about it yet," I responded.

"Olzhas says it is very important moment and he wishes to send me and some Kazakh radiation survivors to attend. He instructed me to ask if you would take us to this meeting. He will send us to New York airport if you can take us on to Nevada," Vladimir explained.

After a short hesitation I responded, "Well, I certainly will make every effort to take your group to Los Vegas for Olzhas. How many people would come? What are the dates of the seminar? How long will your group remain here? And – -- "

The conversation ended as abruptly as it began. I flopped down into my favorite overstuffed chair in disbelief. How in God's name will I ever be able to take eight or ten people across the country to this big gathering? Today is February 5. We will need to drive because I can't imagine finding the money to fly us all. To arrive by April 9, it would be necessary to leave New Jersey around the first of April. Just eight weeks to make all the plans and arrangements. And where will the money come from? Our new organization is still in the beginning stages and we haven't a penny in funds yet. Whatever it costs will have to come out of my pocket again, just as it has the past four years. I just recovered from the cost of our three-week trip to Russia and Kazakhstan last September when we went to their nuclear test site in Semipalatinsk and celebrated the permanent closing with thousands of Kazakhs.

Then I realized – the Honorable Olzhas Suleimenov from the Soviet Kremlin was asking for *my* help. How am I going to accomplish this task without letting him down? This will take a lot of planning, but I am certain I can do the planning part. I love organizing events like this, and I will be participating in the global movement to end nuclear testing. I cannot think of anything more important for me to undertake.

"Oh Lois, I didn't realize you were home," Ana gasped as she walked into my little office space of my apartment.

"Ana, you won't believe who I just spoke to on the phone," I responded.

Ana Aleksandrova arrived in the United States four months ago on a visitor's visa from Sofia, Bulgaria, where she was an assistant professor at the University of Sofia. She is thirty-five, single, has long, thick, dark brown hair and very dark eyes. I met her two months ago and when she told me she needed a place to stay, I offered my second bedroom to her.

I told Ana it will be a very big job to put this trip together. I must keep my day job to finance it and if she wants to help, she is welcome to go with us.

"That would be wonderful. I would get to see so much of the country. I speak a little Russian so I could help with the translating. My brother, Dimitar, is trying to make arrangements to come visit me soon. Could he go with us too?"

"I'm not sure yet, Ana. First we must see exactly how many are coming in Olzhas' delegation. I will rent the largest van possible, which will probably be a twelve-passenger van," I said.

For the next seven weeks, I worked my day job every day and then rushed home and spent until midnight making all the preparations. I didn't have a computer because in 1992, only the wealthiest owned computers, so I had to do all the plans by hand. There was very little internet, and no one had e-mail anyway. There was no such thing as Google, leaving me with little helpful resources. Whenever I needed to type or fax anything, I went to my favorite hangout, Kinko's, on Spring Street here in Princeton.

First, I laid out a large map of the United States on my dining room table and began planning the route. I circled the cities where acquaintances lived whom I figured would help host us for a night. Since we were traveling across the country with no financial help, I had to rely on private families hosting us in their homes, providing a potluck supper when we arrived, feeding us breakfast in the morning, and sending their guests off with lunches in their hands for that day.

Thank God I had traveled thirty-five days across the country back in 1988 on the Soviet–American Peace Walk. I learned a whole lot about host families on that walk, and already had lots of personal contacts and names of peace and religious organizations to call on for help.

I had to use the telephone to make my personal contacts, and in 1992 every long-distance telephone call ate heavily into my funds. There was no such thing as free coast-to-coast calling, so my phone bill for February and March totaled hundreds of dollars. Fortunately for me, the bill didn't come until after I departed on my trek west and I went a month or two without a phone when I returned, until it was paid.

I rented a twelve-passenger van with unlimited mileage and put it on the charge card of a gracious member of our World Citizen Diplomats (WCD), Barbara Rash, one of my closest friends. She owned La Jolie Beauty Salon on Witherspoon Street in Princeton and was one of the twenty people who helped me put together our organization. Barbara offered to charge the van on her card and told me I could pay it off monthly when I returned. Thank God for good friends.

By relying on the host families for all the lodging and meals and putting the van rental and telephone expenses off until I returned, I only needed to come up with cash for the gas, tolls and small daily expenses. When I left New Jersey, gas was .80 cents a gallon, but it went up to .99 cents as we traveled west. Fortunately, all the members of our organization donated to help me with the fuel expenses, which made the trip possible.

Vladimir faxed to my office-away-from-home (Kinko's) the names, ages, and short bios of all eight participants coming in his delegation. He said they would arrive on March 27.

Ana begged me to provide her with an official invitation from our organization for her brother to get a visitor's visa so he could arrive in the states by the middle of March. I agreed. Thus, we now had Vladimir, Olzhas' translator from Russia, seven Kazakh radiation survivors from Kazakhstan, Ana and Dimitra from Bulgaria, and me. Little did I know, while planning the trip, that there would be many moments over the next month when I would feel like the foreigner in my own native country. I had taken a course in beginner Russian three years ago, but after a few months, my Russian instructor told me I would remain a beginner student forever. Since my knowledge of the Russian language was extremely limited, I was blessed with Vladimir, who ended up my translator and partner, sitting right next to me in the front passenger seat. I don't believe I ever allowed him to venture more than a few feet from my side during the whole trip.

The members of our growing little organization planned a nice welcoming dinner for the night our Soviet delegation was to arrive, only to have it postponed four times until the Russian authorities finally agreed to allow the group to leave Moscow. Olzhas had half the Kremlin pulling strings to help him get the permission needed from their stubborn communist bureaucrats to finally get our travelers aboard an Aeroflot airplane heading to the USA.

Rose and Vladimir Herbeck worked with Dolores Hewitt, Fran Morasco, Dietrich and Philomena Fischer, Amadeo D'Adamo, Marge Hornak, Barbara Rash, and my son, Michael Leffler, to plan the welcoming dinner. I refer to these members as my "dependable ten." Dolores and Fran had accompanied me the previous fall to the Semipalatinsk test site, so they were exceptionally excited to host our Kazakh delegation after our remarkable three-week stay in Kazakhstan.

Gigi Callahan offered to have the dinner at her large exquisite home in the outskirts of Princeton. Gigi was thirty-eight years old. She was a member of a wealthy family in Chicago and received a large stipend each month. She was single with one son, aged around twelve. She had never shown an interest in our organization the previous four years, but suddenly became very interested once Ana told her that I had received a call from Olzhas in the Kremlin asking me to take his delegation west. Suddenly Gigi and Ana started asking questions about how we organized and for copies of our by-laws. Never in my wildest dreams would I ever have suspected what these two conniving women were doing behind my back. It took two weeks into our trip before I found out. And it was a whopper!

On March 30, we received the final telephone call informing us that our delegation had finally taken off from Moscow and were on their way.

On Tuesday morning, March 31, I drove our newly rented van to JFK airport to pick up our travelers. I held a big cardboard poster up with Vladimir Iakimets' name on it and stood at the International Arrivals platform in the waiting area to greet our guests. I only knew two of them personally. Vladimir had been with Olzhas when Dolores and I picked them up at Dulles Airport back in December 1990. I knew Yuri Kuiden because he accompanied us on our previous trip last September to the Semipalatinsk test site. He is the Kazakh photojournalist who took all the pictures from that remarkable trip and planned to photograph this trip also.

Yuri's wife, Vera Kuidina, was accompanying him on this trip. She was a prominent organic chemist back in Almaty.

Also, sixty-nine-year-old Alexander Medzerov was among the delegation. He is a famous Soviet poet whose poetry was written in the tradition of Alexander Black. His bio said that Alexander's poetry has been translated into many languages.

The most famous member of the arriving delegation was twenty-four-year-old Karimbek Kuyukov. Karimbek was born near the Semipalatinsk test site. He was born without arms. As a radiation victim, he survived because his family took good care of him and taught him how to use his feet and toes in place of his hands and arms. Before Karimbek was born, his parents had sat in front of their yurt and marveled at the mushroom cloud from the Soviet nuclear tests in the distance, having no idea the radiation from the explosion would cause their baby to be born armless. As a child, Karimbek learned to paint by holding a paint brush in his teeth. He was featured in the March 1992 Sierra Magazine, published a few weeks before they left Moscow. The article was written by Jim Lerager, an American journalist from California who went to Semipalatinsk to investigate and write the story about Karimbek. Karimbek brought many of his paintings with him to put on display as we traveled west. Because Karimbek often needed help, he was accompanied by his twenty-six-year-old sister, Saule Arginbaeva, who attended to him when necessary.

Amantai Kaliev was an environmental activist from Pavlodar, near the Semipalatinsk test site. He was also the chairman of a regional political party that organized the People's Congress of Kazakhstan. He was the main person in charge of hosting our American delegation when we visited their test site last September.

The eighth and final member of our delegation was forty-six-year-old Rollan Seisenbayev. Rollan was a Kazakh writer and playwright. He was the president and founder of the Foundation for the Child Victims of Nuclear Testing and Ecological Catastrophes. He was the first Soviet writer who dared to write about nuclear testing in his autobiographical book, *The Day the World Collapsed.*

As I stood among all the international greeters waiting to welcome their loved ones coming in on the Aeroflot flight from Moscow, I reminisced about my last remarkable trip to Kazakhstan. Soon, a small group walked through the swinging double doors into our arrival hall and I immediately recognized Vladimir and Yuri. Vladimir was the only one of the eight of them who had ever been to the United States, and I could see the excitement on all their faces. I found myself almost as excited as they were.

I led them out of the masses of people and up the elevator to the roof parking lot where I parked our van. Vladimir introduced me to all his comrades, and we packed the van with their luggage. Soon, we were driving west on the Belt Parkway heading for Princeton.

Two hours later, we pulled into the driveway of Gigi's home. We were greeted by all our WCD members and enjoyed their wonderful spread of food and beverages to ward off their exhaustion. It had been a difficult, stressful five days for all of them trying to get out of Russia and on their way to America, the country they never imagined they would see in their lifetime.

Following dinner, while we were discussing how we would pack our van the next morning, I looked around and saw an exhausted group of travelers. I told them to grab their suitcase and go with their host families to get some sleep. I explained that we had a long drive tomorrow and they should get as much rest as possible.

Gigi hosted a big breakfast for all the travelers the next morning. The host families packed each of their guests' big lunches with lots of snacks to carry them through their first day of traveling. After we ate our breakfast, we packed the van. Hugs were abundant as goodbyes were said. Twelve hours in Princeton and already they had many American friends. But the trip hadn't even started yet. They had no idea what they were facing.

It was 6 am by the time I had all my passengers settled in their seats. I passed out a neatly typed packet for each of them with dates, times of arrivals and departures, and names of the organizers and their organizations. Of course, no one except Vladimir and Ana could read English, so for the first couple of hours, Vladimir read each entry and our passengers wrote their own notes in Russian.

"We are on our way to Dayton, Ohio," I told them. When I said we would need to cover 571 miles before evening, they all gasped. In most of their Soviet Republics, Russia and Kazakhstan included, the roads were horrendous with potholes and asphalt bumps and breaks everywhere. Even if you could find a car in good enough shape to go sixty miles an hour, it was impossible to travel very fast because of the condition of the roads. It was not in their realm of imagination to think anyone could go almost 600 miles in one day. However, it only took a few hours into the trip for them to begin to relax and forget their earlier ideas that I was totally out of my mind. It took a few more days for them to begin to believe we could ever keep up with my scheduled projections.

At 6 pm, we pulled into the church parking lot where our host, Cathy Blocker had told me to meet her. She was a member of the SANE/FREEZE organization. Vladimir introduced all our passengers to her, and she said her group members were in the basement, waiting to greet us with dinner. They grabbed their belongings and followed her down the stairs. There is no way to describe the shock and delight on their faces when they entered the big room where about thirty members of her group had laid out a potluck dinner fit for kings.

Following their meal, they exhibited Yuri's photos of nuclear radiation victims in the Semipalatinsk region. Then, Rollan told his story of being evacuated when he was eleven years old with all the people in his village because the hydrogen bomb was about to be tested forty kilometers away on Soviet soil. Karimbek soon stood in front of his audience and told why he was born with no arms. He had fifty or more of his paintings on display and showed the audience how he held a paint brush in his teeth while he painted. The audience were spellbound!

Cathy Blocker had invited her local newspaper to cover the evening's event, so our delegation enjoyed their very first American interview. Little did they know, it was the first of almost a hundred interviews over the next four weeks.

Since our next destination would only involve a 117-mile trek, I told the host families and our group members to enjoy the morning together and that we would meet at the church at 3 pm the next afternoon.

Three o'clock on Thursday afternoon, joyous hugs again ensued, followed by more tearful goodbyes. We departed Dayton, this time heading for Indianapolis, Indiana. We arrived at 6 pm and were greeted by our host, Karen Lipps, who represented the Peace and Justice organization. Again, a lovely potluck supper was waiting for us; speeches followed, and the host families gleefully escorted their new Soviet friends to their homes for the evening.

Eight o'clock on Friday morning, April 3, we left Indianapolis and began our 477-mile-long journey toward Des Moines, Iowa. It was Ed Fallon who greeted us at 6 pm that evening. The members of his organization, the Clairon Alliance, had another tasty potluck waiting for our arrival along with more than fifty excited host families and friends. Following dinner, our delegates presented their two-hour program, which again left all in attendance speechless. Host families were assigned their guests for the night and off our delegation went, for another evening and morning with new American friends.

At 1 pm on Saturday afternoon, we all assembled at the church. Goodbyes were said and off we went, this time heading 194 miles to Kansas City, MO. At 5 pm Thomas Zoellers, the president of the Alliance for Homeless, and Len Cheetum of SANE/FREEZE greeted us at our rendezvous point. Introductions were made and we followed them into their meeting hall where another bountiful dinner was waiting. Speeches followed, host family assignments were made, and before I knew it, all my people were rushed into their waiting cars as if the hosts were giving refuge to the most important Soviets our country had ever captured.

On Sunday morning, April 5, we assembled at 6 am to launch our next long trek – this time 623 miles through Denver to Boulder, Colorado. I believe, by the end of this day, my travelers finally conceded that I knew not only what I was doing when I prepared our itinerary but also how to drive "better than any lady we ever met" – according to Karimbek. Some of those from Kazakhstan had never even ridden in a car before leaving on their trip to Moscow. They walked or rode a horse or a camel. Cars were rarely seen in this region of the world. Buses provided the basic transportation for traveling to another village or town, but Karimbek and Saule lived their whole lives in and around their yorta on the steppes and desert of this very remote region of the world. I could see in my rearview mirror as they stared out the van windows that they were in one major cultural shock during their first two weeks in America.

At 6:30 pm, we arrived at the Rocky Mountain Peace Center in Boulder. Mary Axe of the Sister Cities organization was the first to greet us. Mike Denton of the 100th Monkey and Tom Marshall of the Rocky Mountain Peace Center also welcomed us and following introductions, we were escorted into their reception room where about a hundred citizens were anxiously waiting to meet their interesting guests from far off Russia and Kazakhstan.

To Be Continued. . .

Karimbek with his paintings
and drawings on display at
a speaking engagement.

Karimbek playing a piano with his toes. Taken at the home of one of our Host Families as we traveled around the USA.

<u>*DES MOINES, IOWA:*</u>

Host Ed Fallon of the
"Clarion Alliance"

<u>*MOSCOW, IOWA:*</u> Passing through on our way west.

BOULDER, COLORADO:
Mary Axe. "Sister Cities" was our
organizer and host.

Tom Marshall & LeRoy Moore of the
"Rocky Mountain Peace Center" also
helped with our visit along with Mike
Denton of the "100th Monkey" org.

We held an open-air seminar on the
Campus of the University of Colorado.

TUESDAY ♻ **APRIL 7, 1992**

- Council mulls fireplace restrictions —*page 2*
- Kaye commands kudos —*page 15*

Weather
Sunny with
scattered afternoon
showers
—*page 16*

Colorado Daily

Serving the university community since 1892 — VOL. 100 NO. 61

Nuke-test foes recruit students

Russians speak at Fountain

By CHRIS WOLF
Colorado Daily Staff Writer

Leaders of a movement that has helped stop nuclear testing in the former Soviet Union came to CU Monday to ask students to pressure the U.S. government for a matching moratorium. Standing under the April sun at the UMC fountain, the activists were met by group stoicism worthy of a U.S. arms-control negotiating team.

Dressed in a blue business suit and speaking through an interpreter, a regional director of the movement for bipolar disarmament tried to inspire international solidarity among the students, who tanned and talked, wearing shorts, sandals and sunglasses. Amanthai Kaliev said the "Nevada-Semipalatinsk Movement" is named after the U.S. and former-Soviet states where nuclear tests have been conduct-

[TURN TO PAGE 9]

Page likes job, seeks to retain it

By PETER POCHNA
Colorado Daily Staff Writer

Boulder County Commissioner Homer Page likes his job, and Monday he announced that he wants to keep it for another four years.

"I have really enjoyed being on the board of commissioners," said Page, a Boulder Democrat. "There are a lot of very important issues coming up, and I don't want to leave while I'm in the middle of them. I want to finish them up."

Page's first term in office expires at the end of this year. He was elected to the three-member board in 1988, after serving seven years on the Boulder City Council.

So far, nobody has announced intentions to challenge him for his District 3 seat, which encompasses most of Boulder and much of Boulder County's mountain communities.

[TURN TO PAGE 8]

INSIDE THE DAILY

Yuri Kuidin, photojournalist and president of the Kazakhstan Union of Photographers, displays his pictures of the Nevada nuclear test site. People gathered in the University Memorial Center fountain area on Monday to view his work.

Charlie Johnson/Colorado Daily

Two teams vie for exec slot

Predecessors 'antagonistic'

By KEVIN BLOCKER
Colorado Daily Staff Writer

CU student leaders have been too antagonistic and confrontational with university regents and administrators, and that needs to stop, according to the executive ticket of Ken Bianchi, David Panzer and Brad Holland.

As long as he has been at CU, the student government has always taken a hard-line approach in dealing with CU's hierarchy, said Holland, a former representative of the CU Student Union Legislative Council. Numerous bills, and lawmakers themselves, are always "demanding" something from administration, he said.

Holland and his fellow candidates are running against Christof Kheim, a current executive, Karen Buck and Jeannette Galanis in the April 13-15 UCSU elections.

"Previous (student) administrations certainly haven't developed a rapport with administration in the past," Holland said. "They always do things that alienate administration." He and his running mates believe productive communication can be achieved through diplomacy and tact.

The trio has outlined six additional goals for its campaign platform.

[TURN TO PAGE 3]

Learning environment displeases incumbent

By KEVIN BLOCKER
Colorado Daily Staff Writer

Executive hopefuls Karen Buck, Jeannette Galanis and Christof Kheim say they are not pleased with the learning environment at CU.

If they are elected to office, they said they will work toward establishing better lines of communication between the CU Student Union and CU's administration. They think weak lines between the two groups have alienated the student body.

"The learning environment isn't conducive, and students are recognizing this," Kheim said. He cited the recent controversy concerning CU Head Football Coach Bill McCartney's statements about homosexuality's being "an abomination of Almighty God."

The coach made the statements during a press confer-

[TURN TO PAGE 6]

CHAPTER 7 – PART 2

EDUCATING THE AMERICAN PEOPLE ON THE "HORRORS OF THE MUSHROOM"

Our delegation spent Monday, April 6, enjoying the spring sunshine that engulfed the Boulder community. We held an open-air seminar for the students on the campus of the university, where our exhibitions were displayed, and Rollan sold copies of his book near the fountain at the center of the campus.

That evening, some hundred people attended the potluck supper held in the Mennonite Church, and members of our delegation again shared their individual stories, culminating in a very rewarding evening. The highlight of the day was meeting Ms. Tucker Adams, who spent the past month collecting medicines from all the doctors and pharmacies throughout Boulder and Denver. She took it upon herself to organize the collection of medicines for the children's hospital in Almaty and arranged to send it by military aircraft to Kazakhstan.

Tuesday morning at six o'clock, we departed from Boulder and traveled 365 miles south to Los Alamos, New Mexico – the birthplace of the atomic bomb.

"In 1942, President Franklin Roosevelt directed the Army Corps of Engineers to create the Manhattan Project, and in 1943 Los Alamos was referred to as 'Project Y,'" I began explaining as Vladimir translated.

"Robert Oppenheimer led the lab during World War II, while scientists from all over the world were recruited and hired by the United States Government to work on the Manhattan Project."

"On July 16, 1945, the Trinity Test was conducted, demonstrating that we had the capability to successfully drop a nuclear bomb that would leave the world in shock for decades. Three years of scientific experiments ended on August 6, 1945, when a uranium bomb nicknamed 'Little Boy' was dropped on Hiroshima, Japan. Three days later, on August 9, the second bomb, called 'Fat Man,' was dropped on Nagasaki," I explained.

"Why did the United States drop those two terrible bombs?" Karimbek asked. "They killed so many innocent people."

I replied, "In December 1944, Japan attacked Pearl Harbor in Hawaii and killed thousands of sailors, military personnel, and their families. They also destroyed many American ships. This convinced the United States that Japan had to be stopped, and our leaders knew if we invaded Japan, many more of our soldiers would lose their lives. So, they chose to use these horrible bombs to end the war."

"From 1963 to 1992, many more nuclear bombs were tested by the USA. In 1991 and 1992, the last eight tests were detonated at the Nevada nuclear test site, which we will be visiting in a couple of days outside Las Vegas, Nevada," I continued. "Four of those last eight tests were conducted by the scientists right here, at Los Alamos Labs, and four were conducted by the Lawrence Livermore Labs in California. The American citizens have been trying to close the Nevada test site for many years, and now that you successfully closed your site in Semipalatinsk, the American activists are more determined than ever to close our site too," I concluded.

Soon we were on our way south, arriving at the Albuquerque Center for Peace & Justice and greeted by Sally, Evelyn, and Chris – three members of the group that was hosting us. Our evening meal was held in the Peace Center. It turned out to be a very special evening for me because I hadn't seen my cousin, Steve Perin, in more than thirty-five years. Steve was the eldest of Aunt Edith's five children and I'm the eldest of my family, both of us fifty-five years old. Aunt Edith was my dad's older sister. She married Bob Perin, had five children and they spent their lives in Phoenix, Arizona. I only saw Steve and my other cousins about once every third or fourth year as we grew up, when Aunt Edith and Uncle Bob brought them east to visit.

Steve graduated from Brigham Young University and eventually became a professor there. He married an American Indian woman and had two sons, but as our government's nuclear capabilities increased and the cold war escalated, Steve became paranoid that there would be a nuclear war. Eventually, he took his family to Placida, New Mexico, not too far from Albuquerque, where he moved them into a large cave because he was convinced there would be a catastrophic nuclear war and he wanted them to survive.

Steve's father was a professional National Boy Scout Leader and every summer while growing up, he went to Philmont Boy Scout Camp with his family where his father ran the camp. He found the cave in his youth and spent a lot of time exploring it every summer. It had several spacious rooms and a large entryway, creating lots of light. It was his idea of the perfect place to be safe from a nuclear explosion.

Of course, all his immediate and extended family members became increasingly worried that Steve had lost his mind. Finally, his younger brother, Dan, came to his rescue. Dan bought a cabin very close to the entrance to the cave where Steve and his family were living. Because Dan was living in Ponape, in the far eastern Carolina Islands south of the Philippines, Dan asked Steve to move into the cabin so no one would vandalize it until Dan came back to the States to live.

Thus, Steve moved his family into the cabin, knowing that his family could run back into the cave if ever there was a nuclear nightmare unleashed on the United States.

Steve resembled the perfect picture of a modern "caveman." He had a gray mustache and beard, with a head full of hair. His skin was tanned and somewhat wrinkled by the dry southwestern sun. He displayed a big happy smile and I realized from our conversation that he was in complete control of his senses. We enjoyed a marvelous evening together. He was very impressed with our delegation and to know we were all working hard to end nuclear testing.

Once dinner was over, several group members gave short speeches and then we showed a video I received in the mail the day before we left New Jersey. *Bound by the Wind* was an 88-minute long documentary produced and directed by David L. Brown, a San Francisco documentary filmmaker. The film had just been completed. It depicted the global human impact of nuclear weapons testing and the forty-year international campaign to achieve a comprehensive test ban. It focused on the plight of the world's "downwinders" – those who have been directly affected by radiation from nuclear testing because they lived downwind from the actual testing sites. Consequently, they lost many members of their families to cancer brought on by the exposure to nuclear radiation. Karimbek is one of the "downwinder survivors" whose personal life has been ruthlessly affected because of exposure to the testing site in Semipalatinsk, Kazakhstan.

Seven o'clock Wednesday morning, we left Albuquerque and traveled 448 miles to Tucson, Arizona. It was a sunny late afternoon when we arrived at the city limits. Vladimir was helping me search for our destination when all of a sudden, our whole van erupted into howling laughter.

"Vladimir, what is going on back there?" I asked.

In between his own laughing, Vladimir said, "Karimbek just announced to everyone – 'Now I'm certain we're all in heaven.'" "He's referring to those beautiful trees lining the street with oranges hanging from their branches," Vladimir told me. He explained that oranges are an incredibly special treat in Semipalatinsk and Karimbek had never seen an orange growing before.

Soon we were at our destination and my cousin, Robin Perin, was waiting to greet us. Robin is Steve's younger sister. After high school, she became a nurse and worked ten years in a Tucson hospital. Eventually, she decided to go back to college and study law. Once she earned her law degree, she became the attorney for all the doctors and hospital personnel she once worked with, certainly understanding their professional situations.

Our delegation was very special to Robin because she was actively involved with the Tucson Sister City project. Almaty, Kazakhstan is the sister city to Tucson, Arizona. Robin was also a member of the Physicians for Social Responsibility, so she included the members of both groups to host us.

Robin and the other members of her groups organized a magnificent evening event. Both groups consisted of professionals: doctors, nurses, and anesthesiologists represented the Physicians for Social Responsibility, and the Tucson mayor and several Arizona congressmen represented the Sister Cities program. More than fifty local people attended the evening potluck supper, filling the spacious condominium event room from wall to wall.

Robin made a perfect hostess. Her olive-shaped brown eyes sparkled, and her smile made everyone feel warm and welcome. Living in the southwest provided such a radiant tan that made both her and her brother, Steve, look so healthy. Our whole group enjoyed Tucson immensely and they voted it one of the best experiences of their trip around the country.

In the morning, a lovely breakfast buffet was held on the patio of Robin's condominium complex. There were several newspaper and TV journalists at both evening and morning events, so our delegation was featured on several news channels and in many newspaper articles following our visit. The interview by Channel 4 TV crew was a special highlight of the morning before we hugged our new friends goodbye and boarded our trusty van, heading out to visit the Biosphere-2 Project in Oracle, Arizona.

As we rode toward our destination, I gave Vladimir the information I had gathered regarding the biosphere and he read it aloud to all our van occupants.

"The Biosphere-2 Project is an on-going ecological experiment built as a laboratory for global ecology. It is a tightly sealed glass and steel structure in which scientists have created seven complete eco-systems that mirror those here on earth," Vladimir read.

"On September 26, 1991, eight researchers, known as the Biospherians, sealed the airlock and Biosphere-2 began. It is the world's largest and most complex closed ecological research facility. Mark Nelson and Jane Pointer were the project leaders and in charge of the Agriculture Testing for the intensive, sustainable nonpolluting farming system. The eight participants were expected to remain inside this enclosure for two years with absolutely no help from the outside world," Vladimir concluded.

We arrived at noon and the guide escorting us around the grounds made arrangements for us to meet Mark Nelson and Jane Pointer through the visitor's glass communication window. It was a very special treat to meet Mark and Jane and to see our group enjoy communicating with them.

This was a dream come true for Vladimir because he was a physicist trained in Moscow where he actually worked with Mark on the very beginning stages for building this biosphere years earlier.

By 7 pm, we finally arrived in Phoenix, and Charlotte Marlin representing Mensa greeted us with other members who prepared our evening meal at Charlotte's home.

Friday morning, we departed from Phoenix and embarked upon the next 230-mile trek north through Oak Creek Canyon and Sedona, arriving in time to eat our lunches dangling our feet over the south rim of the breathtaking Grand Canyon. It took all my energy to pry each member away from the spectacular view and pile them into our van so we could move onward west.

Two hundred and fifty miles later, we arrived at the Hoover Dam in time to take pictures before the sun went down behind the mountains.

We arrived in Las Vegas, Nevada an hour later, greeted by Helen Hughes and Reinard Knutsen, both members of the American Peace Test. They introduced us to our host families, who whisked everyone off to their homes for dinner.

Saturday and Sunday were crammed with excitement from morning until evening. I picked up everyone at their host family homes, and by 7 am, we were driving out into the desert thirty miles from Las Vegas. There was a Peace Camp set up by the American Peace Test organization, which sponsored this nuclear disarmament event pressing for a moratorium to end all nuclear testing.

We were provided with a large tent where Yuri displayed all his photographs of the radiation victims in Kazakhstan, Karimbek displayed all his paintings and sketches he had done holding a paint brush or pencil in his teeth, and Rollan had his books on display.

There were thousands of people in attendance both days. Pictures were taken and many interviews by newspapers, radio, and TV stations were conducted almost hourly. My little delegation had become famous overnight.

The first famous person we were introduced to was Casey Kasem, who was serving as the Master of Ceremonies both days. Mr. Kasem was a dark-haired, handsome, happy-go-lucky man of Lebanese American heritage, who became famous as the host of the American Top 40 Hit Parade radio program that debuted on July 4, 1970. His show soon became one of the most popular syndicated radio shows not only in the USA but also all around the world. From 1980 to 1990 the TV show, America's Top 10, featured him as its host.

Around noon, our delegation was invited to enjoy lunch at the home of one of the local host families, where Vladimir and I were seated next to a slightly built white-haired man introduced to us as Professor Daniel Ellsberg. Our host explained to us that Daniel graduated from Harvard in the 50s and served as an officer in the Marines. When he returned from Vietnam, he was hired by the Rand Corporation and in 1964, was sent to work in the Pentagon.

In 1967, he led a top-secret study of classified documents regarding the conduct of the Vietnam war, and in 1968 those documents became known as the Pentagon Papers. Because he held an extremely high-level security clearance, he had access to the complete set of documents which revealed that the government had knowledge all along that the war could not be won and the continuance would lead to many more causalities than was ever admitted publicly. The papers also showed that high-ranking officials had a deep cynicism toward the public and a total disregard for the loss of life and injury suffered by soldiers and civilians.

He secretly made copies of the Pentagon Papers and approached several senators, including Senator William Fulbright and Senator George McGovern, to release the papers on the Senate floor. They flatly refused! On Sunday, June 13, 1971, *The New York Times* published the first of nine excerpts. Immediately, the Nixon Administration prevented *The Times* from publishing the other eight articles. Therefore, Ellsberg leaked the documents to *The Washington Post* and seventeen other newspapers, who also released the first excerpt. On June 30, the Supreme Court ordered publication to resume freely.

The release of these papers led to a trial of Daniel Ellsberg on charges under the Espionage Act of 1917, carrying a maximum sentence of 115 years. Due to gross government misconduct and illegal evidence gathering, the judge dismissed all charges in May 1973, and Daniel Ellsberg became an instant whistleblower hero.

Since then, Ellsberg has been arrested in nonviolent civil disobedience more than fifty times at Rocky Fiats Nuclear Weapons Production Facility, the Nevada Test site, the Lawrence Livermore Nuclear Weapons Design Facility, and the Vandenberg Missile Test site. He is one of the many famous Americans committing civil disobedience against the continuing nuclear weapons tests.

Vladimir and I had a very informative discussion with Prof. Ellsberg and the professor thanked us for all our effort to bring the truth to the American people.

On Saturday afternoon, our delegation members participated in a panel discussion at Las Vegas University, following David Brown's introduction of his documentary, *Bound by the Wind*.

That early evening, I met Jeffrey See, an activist from California who informed me there was a lady, Dottie Troxell, who desperately wanted to meet with Karimbek on our trip back east. She asked that we meet her in Kansas City, MO. I told him to relay a message to her that we would arrive in Kansas City on Wednesday evening, April 22, and would be hosted by Len Cheetum, the president of SANE/FREEZE who organized our stay coming west.

On Palm Sunday, Karimbek, Amantai, and Vladimir served as panelists at the GANA (Global Anti-Nuclear Alliance) roundtable discussion. Interviews by local TV and radio stations followed and David Brown recorded a lengthy interview to add to his documentary.

Monday morning, we departed from Las Vegas and arrived in San Marcos by noon, California. My eldest daughter, Debbie, greeted us along with my five grandchildren who lived in Oceanside. My beautiful red-headed daughter arranged a speaking engagement for all her Soviet guests at the Vista Washington Elementary School, attended by three of my grandchildren. We divided into two groups, composed of five in each group. Vladimir and Evelina served as the two translators. Each group gave three forty-five-minute presentations throughout the upper grades of the school. It was in the 90s and the sun was beating down. There was no air-conditioning in the school, so everyone was totally exhausted by 3 pm when our afternoon commitment ended. Everyone ran for our van and gave sighs of relief as the air-conditioning blasted on high. The first thing that came to my mind, though, was how difficult it will be for my travelers to adapt to their homeland again, without all these comforts we are enjoying while traveling.

We followed Debbie to the rendezvous point where all her host families were patiently waiting to meet and run away with their new visitors for a lovely evening at their homes. As for Karimbek, Saule, Rollen, and me, we followed Debbie to her home where we enjoyed a swim and cookout and I enjoyed a long-awaited visit with my grandchildren.

On Tuesday, April 14, we spent the morning on the California beach and the afternoon visiting San Diego. The highlight of the evening was a surprise fifty-fifth birthday party hosted by Debbie, her husband, Glen, and my grandchildren. What a marvelous way to end our visit to their home in California.

Wednesday, we left at 7 am for Santa Monica where we were greeted by Joe Broido. Joe had organized an opportunity for us to meet the mayor of Santa Monica. We spent two hours sharing stories of what our mission comprised of here in the United States. After the meeting with the mayor, Joe introduced everyone to their new hosts and they spent an enjoyable day and evening visiting Hollywood, Santa Monica, and all the surrounding sites.

Thursday morning at eight o'clock, we departed from Santa Monica and began our drive north along the coast. Our goal was 340 miles away in Livermore, California.

To Be Continued . . .

LOS ALAMOS NATIONAL LABS, NEW MEXICO;

TOP & BOTTOM:
Group members in front of a local store.

CENTER:
Enjoying a lunch break as we travel. Usually our host families from the previous night packed us a lunch.

ALBUQUERQUE, NEW MEXICO:

TOP: Lois and Steve Perin, first cousins who hadn't seen each other in more than 30 years.

BOTTOM: Our display of Yuri Kuiden's photographs

TUCSON, ARIZONA:

TOP: (left to right) Lois with a Tucson resident who was origionally from Kazakhstan, and Robin Perin, Lois' cousin.

MIDDLE: Vladimir speaking to the group who greeted us the evening we arrived.

BOTTOM: Vera and Lois with some of our Tucson hosts.

ORACLE, ARIZONA:

April 9th: Visited the Biosphere 2 Project.

ORACLE, ARIZONA:

April 9th: Visited the Biosphere 2 Project.

Mark Nelson, Biosphere Project Leader was
residing within the biosphere with 6 others
for two years. Jane Pointer and Mark spoke
with us through the glass window.

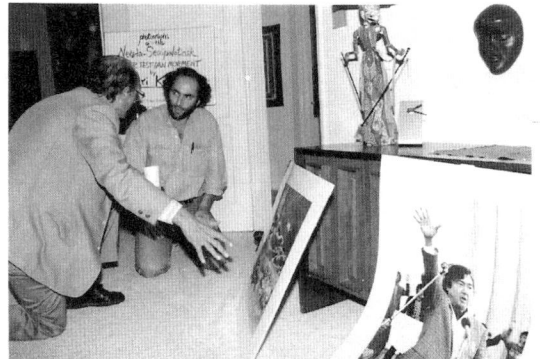

PHOENIX, ARIZONA:

LAS VEGAS, NEVADA:

April 10 – 13: Participated in the four-day gathering sponsored by the "American Peace Test" and the "Nevada Desert Experience" organizations at the Nevada Nuclear Testsite – pushing for a moratorium to stop nuclear testing.

TOP: Lois and Vladimir talking with Casey Kasem. Casey was the Master of Ceremonies for the four-day event.

MIDDLE: Participant in discussion with Shoshone Indians.

BOTTOM: A Chief of the Shoshone Nation speaking with House of Representatives Mike Kopetski at the gathering.

LAS VEGAS, NEVADA:

SAN MARCUS & OEANSIDE, CA:

April 13 – 14:

TOP: Celebrating my birthday.

BOTTOM: Visiting my daughter, Debbie and her family in their home in Oceanside.

CHAPTER 8 – PART 3

EDUCATING THE AMERICAN PEOPLE ON THE "HORRORS OF THE MUSHROOM"

As we continued our journey, we were driving along the boardwalk in Santa Monica when suddenly, the van began to rock with excitement. Everyone was yelling "stop, stop, let us out!" As I searched for a safe spot to pull over, I asked Vladimir why they wanted to get out. He said they just saw Mitch Buchanon and Shauni McCain running on the boardwalk with their famous "*Baywatch* swimsuits on." Of course, I had no idea what they were talking about.

"What is *Baywatch* and how would they know anything about it?"

"Lois, *Baywatch* is a famous TV show about life on the Pacific California boardwalk. They love the show and watch it all the time back in Kazakhstan. It's their favorite American show," Vladimir informed me.

They all jumped out and ran along the boardwalk searching for their favorite TV actors and actresses. It took me another fifteen minutes to collect and entice them back into their seats. Now they were really a happy bunch of travelers. Vladimir said they can't wait to get home and tell everyone that they ran on the same boardwalk the *Baywatch* characters run on.

The drive north along the Pacific Ocean road was spectacular. As we passed through each west coast town, I told my passengers everything I knew about each one. We drove through Ventura, Santa Barbara, Malibu, Monterey, Santa Cruz, and Pala Alto as we made our way to Livermore.

At five o'clock that evening we arrived in Livermore, where we were greeted by Jackie Cabasso and the other members of C.A.R.E. and the Western States Legal Foundation. Yuri and Karimbek put on display many of their pictures, paintings, and drawings and Rollan put his books out. Following the welcoming potluck, they gave their speeches and soon afterward, they were whisked off by their new host families. Tonight is their fifteenth night in America and their twelfth host family.

Morning started early because the Good Friday Sunrise Service began at the crack of dawn, followed by a rally near the Livermore Labs. The Lawrence Livermore National Labs is a premier laboratory which designed and tested nuclear weapons. It was created to sustain and promote American science and technology during the Cold War.

The rally was led by the Jesuit priest, Father Daniel Berrigan. Father Daniel believed war did not solve anything and he went to prison over and over again in defense of his beliefs. Both he and his brother, Father Phillip Berrigan, were famous peace makers, war resisters and truth tellers. Father Phillip was a Roman Catholic priest who became an internationally renowned peace activist and Christian anarchist. Both brothers became famous as part of the

Plowshares Eight. In September 1980, they entered and did damage to the nuclear missile division of General Electric in King of Prussia, PA. The trials went on for ten years and finally, in 1990, the eight were paroled.

After the rally our delegation was again interviewed, this time by CNN who conducted numerous segments of interviews all morning and aired a five-minute spot worldwide the next day on the CNN Headline News Channel. When Vladimir talked with Olzhas, we found out the whole Kremlin saw the segment on their TV.

An hour after departing from Livermore we arrived in San Francisco. We were greeted by Andrea and Evert Kraai. Andrea and Evert accompanied our WCD delegation to Kazakhstan last September when we celebrated the permanent closing of the Soviet nuclear test site. They knew Yuri Kuiden because he traveled with us as the photojournalist for the entire three weeks we were in his country. Now they were anxious to show their appreciation by hosting him in their city.

Andrea was in her thirties. She had dark brown hair that framed her attractive face, accentuating her big brown eyes and exuberant smile. Evert was tall and handsome. He also had lots of wavy brown hair and a genuine smile that I'm certain melted every woman's heart. They made such a handsome couple.

Saturday, we spent the morning touring San Francisco with our host families. Then we were treated to a yacht excursion on the San Francisco Bay, followed by a lavish reception at the home of Professor Hartmut Fischer.

Professor Hartmut Fischer received his PhD from the University of California in Berkeley. He was a professor in the graduate program of economics at the University of San Francisco. He was very interested in the emerging new country of Kazakhstan regarding international trade, finance, and the development of economics.

At three o'clock in the afternoon, we were invited to join more than forty others for an early dinner, held at the San Francisco World Affairs Center, followed by speeches by our delegation.

By five o'clock, we departed from San Francisco to head back to Las Vegas. We drove for nine hours, arriving after midnight and greeted by our previous hosts who were patiently waiting to host us again.

April 19 was Easter Sunday. We were encouraged by the American Peace Test Organization before we left Las Vegas the previous week, to return on Easter and participate in the big Easter Sunday Service and nuclear moratorium rally at the Peace Camp.

After only five hours of sleep I showered, ate a quick breakfast, and warmed up our trusty van. I drove around picking up our delegation members from their host family homes and as we started out to the Peace Camp, we stopped to fill our gas tank. I decided to call home from the telephone booth at the filling station to talk with my son, Michael, and my friend Barbara Rash. We only spoke once a week, usually on Sundays.

Mike answered the phone. As soon as I heard his voice, I knew something was wrong.

"Mike, what's wrong? Did something happen to someone in our family?"

"No mom, but Barbara is going to tell you what happened," Mike said as he handed Barbara his phone.

"Lois, you had better sit down. What we are about to tell you is going to be very shocking," Barbara said.

As I listened to her words, I stood there in disbelief. Of course, I have heard of such a thing happening, but never in my wildest dreams did I ever think it would happen to me and my organization. This kind of thing only happens in Russia!

Barbara continued, "Lois, last night Gigi called together all the Board of Directors, members of World Citizen Diplomats (WCD), except Michael and me. We had no idea what was happening until Rose Herbeck called us when she and Vladimir got home from the meeting. Dolores called us also as soon as we hung up from Rose.

"Both Rose and Dolores told us the same story. Once the eight members of the board arrived at Gigi's home, she passed out a form for each member to sign, stating that they were releasing you as President and Executive Director of WCD. Gigi even had her personal lawyer at the meeting to answer any legal questions we might have. Gigi said you were not a responsible person and had to be released immediately of your position.

"Dolores asked what grounds Gigi had to think you weren't responsible, and Gigi said you ruthlessly accepted the responsibility of taking this international group of people around the United States without going through legal channels. She said if you have an accident our organization would be destroyed."

Barbara continued, "Rose explained to Gigi that our Board of Directors voted to host the delegation and gave you permission to take them on the trip. Rose also explained that it was your initiative that brought us all together and founded the group and you did all the planning and paperwork that got us the 501(c) (3). Then Rose asked Gigi what she wanted to do, destroy everything we had all done for the past three years?"

Mike took the phone from Barbara to give her a chance to catch her breath.

Mike continued, "Gigi's response was staggering. She said WCD was a much-needed organization in the world, and she would sacrifice the time and financial resources to build it into a leading NGO. She said Ana Aleksandrova agreed before the van left Princeton that she would be happy to serve as the President if Gigi would work with her as the Executive Director. Gigi said with Ana's position as President and Gigi's financial resources, they would be able to do so much more than you could ever do.

"Of course, this infuriated every member of the board. By then, they realized that Gigi and Ana had been planning this for more than three weeks. *They had been secretly planning a coup!* All eight of the board members ripped up the forms and left in disgust.

"Mom, what are you going to do with Ana?" my son asked. "Don't lose your temper, Mom. Whatever you do will definitely get back to Olzhas in the Kremlin," Michael concluded with great concern.

"I'm standing here in shock, Mike. How could this woman plan such a thing with Gigi and then spend the past *nineteen days* traveling with me? What audacity she had to ask me to sponsor her brother into the country and for the two of them to travel on this trip without so much as paying one penny! I housed her in my home, for God's sake. I am furious. I want to tear her hair out one strand at a time, and then scratch her eyes out of their sockets. What do you think I'm going to do? I'm tempted to beat the crap out of her," I screamed.

"Mom, please don't. You need to think like the peacemaker you are working so hard to be. Rise above this. Just bring her home and then never have anything more to do with them. The Board of

Directors all stood behind you, and I'm sure they want you to handle this with diplomacy," my sensible, gentle son told me.

Once we hung up, I stood there deciding how I should handle this. I really did feel good that my organization stood behind me all the way. After thinking for several minutes, I calmly walked over to the van where my ten passengers were snuggled in their seats. I entered the van and found Ana sitting directly behind my driver's seat, perched like a peacock on her throne.

"Ana, please step out of the van," I said.

She looked at me, at Vladimir, and at her brother, as she hesitated to move. I stepped up to her, took hold of her upper arm and yanked her out of her seat as she stumbled down the van steps. I spent the next five minutes giving her a good tongue-lashing, never once taking enough of a breath to allow her a moment to respond. The other nine faces were plastered to the windows of the van. That is when I realized that every person in my van probably knew since we left New Jersey what she and Gigi were planning.

I told her I would transport her brother back to Princeton if he so chose, but she could find herself another ride, or walk back.

I jumped in the van and closed the door as I started the engine. Everyone in the van was silent. Ana stood outside, tears flowing.

I told Vladimir what Barbara and Michael told me and when I repeated the word "coup" my whole van gasped. That was one word Soviets knew well.

Finally, Vladimir said, "Lois, I understand fully how you feel. I honestly do not blame you, but Olzhas will be so unhappy with me for letting such a thing happen on our very important mission. He will feel that this will put disgrace on everything we have accomplished.

Please, for the sake of our mission to inspire a moratorium, please just let her ride home."

I knew this was the right thing to do, but I planned to make her suffer as long as possible and to really put a scare in her. After several minutes, I opened the door of the van and said to her, "I'll allow you to ride home, but you're to sit in the last seat of the van the rest of the trip and you will not translate for any interviews or represent our mission in any way. You are no longer a member of our delegation, but just a passenger."

This was not the first time I was betrayed since I became active in my peacemaking years, but it was a real eye-opener to be stabbed in the back by someone I had extended my hand to in friendship.

The Easter Sunday Service at the Peace Camp was led by all our famous peacemakers: Daniel Ellsberg, the Berrigan Brothers, and Casey Kasem. Thousands of others also attended.

Following the service, our delegation members were interviewed by many local and national TV stations, radio programs and newspapers.

At 11 am, the rally was held at the barbed-wire fence bordering the Nevada nuclear test site, and thousands participated in civil disobedience. No one in our delegation participated in the actual act of disobedience, but instead we served as their support group. Memories flashed through my head of my first civil disobedience at this very same location two years earlier. I wanted so much to be out there with the other activists, but naturally this was one I had to sit out. Driving my delegation was my top priority today.

By one o'clock in the afternoon, we departed from Las Vegas and drove 410 miles southeast to Tucson, AZ, where our previous hosts greeted us with private dinners at their homes and hosted us for one more night.

Monday morning, we departed from Tucson at five o'clock and I drove for eighteen hours straight, stopping only for gas and restroom breaks. At dusk, as we were entering Plano, Texas, the speed limit dropped from eighty mph to sixty-five. Unfortunately, I missed the new speed limit sign and not more than fifty feet after it, I heard a siren behind me. Everyone in the van was sleeping until they heard the siren, which scared them all half to death.

The patrolman looked over my credentials and I tried in vain to explain that the speed limit was still eighty. He told me to turn around and I could see the sign about fifty feet behind us with the sixty-five-speed limit. In other words, this was a speed trap. He wrote me a speeding ticket for going fifteen miles over the limit and said I had to appear in court on Thursday evening. I explained that I had to get back east before then, so he said I had to pay him a $100 fine cash on the spot or he would keep my driver's license until I showed up in court. So naturally, I had to pay the fine.

We soon arrived at the home of Jo Ann, our new host coordinator in Plano, who led me around to each host family home where I dropped off their exhausted guests. It was after eleven o'clock at night. We had driven almost a thousand miles and once my head hit the pillow, I didn't wake up for almost twelve hours. I was totally exhausted. Fortunately, I knew when planning the itinerary that it would be a tough ride from Tucson to Plano. Since I didn't have any contacts between the two cities, I had planned on the long trip and then spending this day just resting. I still remember resting that entire day.

By six o'clock Wednesday morning, I felt like a million dollars again. I picked up my passengers from their host homes and we were on our way. Five hundred miles later we arrived in Kansas City, MO, at four in the afternoon. Len Cheetum greeted us for the second time in eighteen days. He escorted us to their bountiful potluck supper and introduced us to all his hosts and to Dottie Troxell.

Dottie was a very nice-looking lady somewhere in her late fifties. She had long grayish-white hair that she pulled back into a neat bun. She wore a purple sweat suit, zipped high at her neck, and a black sleeveless velvet vest, accentuated by large black earrings decorated with rhinestones. Her reading glasses hung from a beaded chain around her neck. She had intense eyes that somehow spoke for the pain she had been through, but her smile helped to display her pleasant personality and wisdom far beyond her years.

Dottie told us her unbelievable story. She worked for more than twenty years at a factory that exposed its workers to radiation. She wore all the regulation attire issued to her and the other workers to supposedly protect them from harm. However, over the years she began to feel sick. She told her supervisor, who informed his boss. She said she had seen her family practitioner who advised her to see an internal specialist. When the boss heard this, he informed Dottie that they had a company hospital in Texas. He told her that her company would pay all her expenses if she agreed to go to their hospital where they had the best internal specialists in the country. The boss assured her there wouldn't be any cost to her.

Thus, like any good patriotic American citizen, Dottie followed her employer's request and flew to Texas for an examination. During her exam, the doctor informed her that he would like to take X-rays and other tests. She agreed. After the initial tests, the doctor told her he wanted to make a tiny one-inch incision so he could do a biopsy of her liver. He told her he would use a local anesthetic to help her relax for a few minutes, and he assured her she wouldn't have any pain or remember a thing afterward.

While they were prepping her, she noticed an anesthesiologist and three other surgically dressed surgeons enter the room. She said she remembered looking at the wall clock. She tried to ask the nurse why so many people were there, but they immediately put her to sleep. When she woke up and could read the clock on the wall, she was shocked. She had been out for almost three hours, and she was in extreme pain. Instead of a one-inch incision she had a ten-inch incision across her entire abdomen. They kept her in the recovery room for two days, sedated. When she asked the doctor what happened, he said it became necessary to do more extensive surgery, but that she would be fine now.

When she arrived home, she was still in terrible pain. She went to her family doctor, who had been her doctor since she was in her twenties. He ran several tests and then called her to bring her son and come to his private office.

When they arrived, the doctor informed Dottie that when she was in the Texas hospital, they had opened her up and took biopsies of all her internal organs. He actually speculated that from what he could see, they were checking to see how much radiation each organ had absorbed since she worked at their factory. In other words, she had been used as a human guinea pig without her permission.

When Dottie confronted her bosses, they denied such a thing ever happened and did everything they could to make her out to be "losing her mind." Dottie went to several newspapers who wrote her accusations, but her bosses simply responded that she was a "crazy old lady." Then Dottie spent months searching for other victims of similar situations and started putting a notebook together. When we met with her, the notebook was more than three inches thick with all kinds of documentation. She handed me the book, and I was shocked at all the information she had gathered.

Before we left Dottie said to me, "Lois, I cannot thank you enough for bringing Karimbek here so I could meet him. Now I feel fulfilled. I will treasure the pictures we took tonight. Karimbek is a radiation victim of his Soviet government, and I am a radiation victim of my employer, who is linked to my American government. I decided to build a Radiation Victims Museum on my property next to our home here in Lexington, MO. I have already started the process to dedicate my land for this project. I hope to have the ground dedication in two to three weeks. Would you please come out for my dedication ceremony? This would make me very happy," Dottie said.

"Of course, I will, Dottie. I will make every effort to come out for it," I told her.

Thursday morning, we left Kansas City and headed east. Five hundred miles later we arrived in Greenfield, Indiana, where my dearest and closest friends, Dan and Sarah McGraw, greeted us. By six o'clock, I had all my passengers delivered to their hosts' homes and I was able to enjoy a quiet evening with Dan and Sarah. They had been my best friends for the last five years that I spent in Indiana, and we remained friends these past ten years in spite of the 700 miles now separating us.

At 4 am Friday, we departed from Indianapolis and headed straight for NYC. Because of the constant publicity throughout the past twenty-four days, every news agency was now interested in my little group of Soviet radiation victims. My office phone in Princeton started receiving messages from every network once the five-minute

CNN special hit TV. Fortunately, I had arranged for Michael and Barbara to check my messages periodically and when I arrived at Dan and Sarah's home, they called me with unbelievable news. The McNeil/Lehrer Newshour TV show wanted an interview. Since Barbara and Mike knew we were arriving home Friday afternoon, they returned their call and set up an appointment for Friday evening at the Regency Hotel across from Central Park in NYC at 6 pm. Thank God we didn't hit any traffic jams or speed traps as we traveled east.

At 5:30 pm we arrived at the hotel where Barbara, Michael, and Dolores were all waiting for us. McNeil/Lehrer news station had a suite reserved and we had a few minutes to freshen up. We planned on Karimbek and Rollan being interviewed and Vladimir translating. Of course, everyone wanted to be filmed, but Mr. Lehrer wanted only the two actual surviving victims.

For more than two hours Mr. Lehrer interviewed them, taking breaks every ten or fifteen minutes to wipe the sweat from their faces and foreheads. The lights for the camera were hot and blinding, causing dehydration and exhaustion. By the time the interview was over, I could see how drained all three of my passengers were. They laid in silence with their eyes closed the entire hour-and-a-half ride back to Princeton. I am certain they weren't sleeping. Instead, they were reliving the remarkable experience they just went through but were too exhausted to even keep their eyes open.

The weekend was spent with the host families, just resting, and recuperating from the twenty-four-day, 8,000-mile excursion around the USA.

Monday, we left in the wee hours of the morning for Washington D.C., where our delegation met with numerous senators and congressmen from 9 am to 9 pm.

Tuesday, we spent the day touring the Big Apple, and Wednesday we spent the whole day lying on the sand at the Jersey Shore and soaking up the warm spring sunshine.

Six o'clock Thursday morning came much too soon for all of us. Our delegation gave hugs and kisses to all their WCD acquaintances who were now their closest American friends forever. Michael, Barbara, and I drove them to JFK and waited with them until their flight was called – heading first from the USA to Moscow to meet with Olzhas and the other People Deputies at the Kremlin; then on to Almaty, the capital of Kazakhstan; and finally from Almaty to Pavlodor and a four-hour bus ride through the desert to their yurt in Semipalatinsk.

On Friday, May 1, thirty days and more than 9,000 miles later, Michael and I washed my rented trusty van.

"Not a nick or scratch on it anywhere, Mom," Michael said.

I thought for a few minutes and then said, "Michael, I'm going to A-1 Limousine Company here in Princeton and putting my application in for a driver position. Certainly, if I can drive across country and back without so much as a scratch on my van, I can surely drive a limo," I said as we both laughed.

I returned the van and drove straight to A-1 Limo, where I was hired that day.

When I got back to my apartment, I tried calling Dottie Troxell again. I had been trying her every day since we returned home, but she didn't answer my calls or return them. It was eight days since we met, and I was planning to drive out next week to attend her groundbreaking dedication ceremony for her Radiation Survivors Museum. I could not understand why she didn't at least return my calls, so I called Jeffrey See in California. Jeffrey was Dottie's friend who arranged our meeting. Fortunately, he gave me his business card when I met him in Las Vegas.

"Hello Jeffrey, this is Lois Nicolai from New Jersey. Thank goodness you were home to receive my call," I said.

We exchanged greetings and I told him about the interview with McNeil/Lehrer and about our farewell at JFK yesterday.

"Jeffrey, thank you so much for arranging for Dottie Troxell and Karimbek to meet. We spent a marvelous evening together in Kansas City. She is a remarkable lady. I am planning to go out to her hometown to attend her dedication of a Radiation Survivors Museum next week, but I can't seem to catch her at home and she isn't returning my calls," I told him.

"Lois, you haven't heard what happened, have you?" There was a long pause before he continued.

"Dottie is dead, Lois. She was found by her son lying on her front lawn. Her riding mower was lying on its side, several feet from her body, and her head was severed and found four feet from her body."

"Oh my God, Jeffrey, this is horrible!" I cried out.

"The worst part is that her son is certain this was no accident. Dottie has been mowing that same lawn with that same mower for more than ten years. She drove tractors in the fields all her life, and never had an accident of any kind. He is certain she could not have lost control of it, and even if she had – it would never have done this. He believes it was a company or government assassination," Jeffrey said.

"But the sheriff has declared it an accident," Jeffrey concluded.

I was crying so hard, I couldn't talk. I told him I had to hang up. I sat there in complete shock. How could such a thing ever happen? Was this an accident – or could this have been an assassination?

August 1992: McNeil/Lehrer News Hour ran the twenty-five-minute segment on Nuclear Testing and the Horrors of Nuclear Radiation, featuring Karimbek Kuikov and Rollan Seisenbayev. Soon after this segment ran, the Nuclear Testing Moratorium Bill was reluctantly signed by President Bush because the authors of the Hatfield Amendment attached it to his "Star Wars" bill, and President Bush did not want to lose his "Star Wars" project. The Soviet Union stopped testing first and the USA now stopped also. Soon after this, China finally stopped their nuclear testing, too, at their Lop Nor, Chinese testing site.

<u>SAN FRANCISO BAY, CA:</u>

April 14 – 18:

Hosts: Andrea and Evert Kraai

TOP: Dottie Troxell, Lexington, MO, USA and Karimbek Kuyukov, Semipalatinsk, Kazakhstan. Two radiation survivors meeting for the first and only time on April 22, 1992, in Kansas City, MO. Karimbek was born with no arms because his parents were exposed to Soviet nuclear testing before his birth. Dottie was exposed to nuclear radiation at the American company she worked for during her adult years.
BOTTOM: Dottie and her son. Dottie was found two weeks after these pictures were taken. She was found by her son after "supposedly" having fell off the riding lawnmower she had driven every summer for many years, and her head was severed! During our meeting with Dottie she informed us that she had been used as a "human guinea-pig" by her company and our government, who were both covering up the seriousness of radiation disease. They coerced her into having surgery for pain she was experiencing, at which time they took biopsies of all her internal organs. She had her family doctor document what had been done to her without her knowledge and she was in the process of exposing this information through the press. Was this an accident (which her son and others said could not have been) or an assassination?

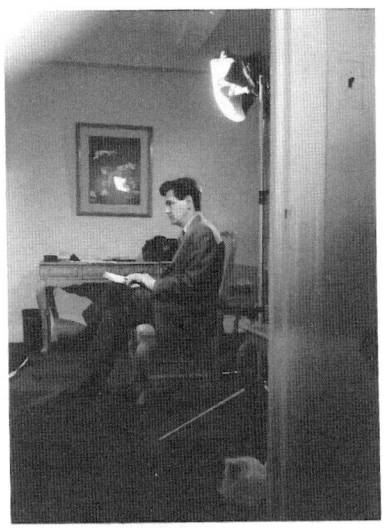

April 24: Karimbek and Rollen were interviewed by McNeal/Lear Newshour on TV. The 20 minute segment was aired nationally in July, 1992 and helped convince the United States Senate to vote for a nuclear disarmament moratorium to stop nuclear testing in Nevada later that summer.

Ex-Soviets take activism to U.S.

In Princeton to push nuke test ba

By MICHAEL JENNINGS
Staff Writer

PRINCETON BOROUGH — To hear them tell it, the only one unaware of the Cold War's conclusion is the United States government. They ask why $13 billion will be spent developing new American nuclear weapons, and why nuclear weapons are still being tested in Nevada.

The questions were raised at a reception held yesterday by World Citizen Diplomats for anti-nuclear protesters from former communist-bloc countries.

The delegates, members of Nevada-Semipalatinski, an anti-nuclear group formed in February 1989, plan a monthlong cross-country tour of 19 cities. They will share experiences they claim brought an end to nuclear testing in the former Soviet Union.

As of yesterday, only two of the expected 15 members of the group had made their way to Princeton. Undaunted, and hopeful that the rest of the contingent will arrive today and tomorrow, trip coordinator Lois Nicolai said the group's plans remain intact.

Nicolai, president of World Citizen Diplomats, will help drive the group to California and back.

"Due to the breakup of the Soviet Union, not all of the embassies in the new republics are fully organized," Nicolai said. "We will probably have to skip a few things on Monday, but we will attend Tuesday's Department of Energy seminar at Georgetown University."

Yuri Kuidin and his wife, Vera Kuidina, of the Republic of Kazakhstan were the only group members to arrive on schedule. Semipalatinski, within Kazakhstan, was the site of 600 Soviet nuclear tests over 40 years before citizen unrest led to an end to the testing, according to Nicolai and the Kuidinas.

THEY SAID they have not come to America to criticize its government but rather to share their experiences and their hope that a worldwide ban on nuclear testing will become a reality.

'They seem rather amazed that a citizens movement in the old Soviet Union could bring about an end to testing there, while it can't here

— Jack Sha
retired Air Force colo

Earlier this year, only the Un States and Britain opposed a Un Nations' resolution calling for su ban, Nicolai said. All of Britain's ing is done at Nevada's Mercury Site, she said.

Yuri Kuidin is a well-known tographer whose book of lands photographs was recently publi in the United States. He has him a series of photographs de ing the results of radiation dis including children born armie with only one eye.

This collection will travel wit group, and will be displayed Ap to May 3 at Merrill Lynch Co ence Center in Plainsboro.

"They seem rather amazed t citizens movement in the old S Union could bring about an e testing there, while it can't b Jack Sharp of Holland, Pa., Sharp, a retired Air Force co also said Congress has appropr $13 billion to develop new nu weapons solely to please the tary-industrial complex.

The Nevada-Semipalatinski nization was founded by Olzh leimenov, a former people's d from Kazakhstan. Putting asic prepared text during a televisi dress, he said the governmen been lying to the people of Ka stan about the health threat levels of radiation, and he call a public meeting to be held th lowing day.

THE MEETING was held o on a frigid day with 5,000 peo tending, Nicolai said. The Sovi ernment did make public corr formation about health da Later tests were canceled w general strike was threatened the republic.

The Times, Trenton, NJ, March 30, 1992

Anti-nuclear activists' Peace Train stops in Princeton

By Regina McAloney
Special Writer

CHAPTER 9 – PART 1

AN UNEXPECTED INVITATION FROM A VERY FAMOUS LADY

As I swung my dazzling shiny Cadillac sedan out of our company parking lot and onto the main street, my attention was drawn to the magnificently landscaped hills bordering Canal Pointe. After all these years, I still favor Canal Pointe as my favorite housing development in all of Princeton. The flowers and shrubbery were always pruned to perfection, but today they appeared to display a special sparkle under the early warm June sun. Maybe it was because they were accentuated by the newly mowed velvety green grass growing all around them.

I had just completed my first month working for A-1 Limousine Company in Princeton. Before I was hired, I asked the owner what I could do to get lots of hours, considering there were 156 drivers and only two were women. Mr. Starr's answer was blunt: "If you want hours, Lois, you need to sign up as my 3 am driver." "And get your bus license," was added with a twinkle in his eye.

I wasn't looking forward to getting up in the middle of the night to go to work, but if that was what it would take to get the hours I wanted, I decided to agree to his terms. The bus license didn't worry me. Driving came naturally and I had driven a leased bus out in Indiana years earlier to transport my teenage workers to the Pioneer Corn Fields each summer. It took only days for me to become one of A-1's most valuable drivers, and I was in my glory!

It was just approaching noon and I was now headed to JFK airport to pick up my passengers coming in from Frankfurt, Germany. Our orders from our company were always very sparse on personal information regarding people we were picking up, so all I knew was that I would be picking up three passengers at the International gate of Continental Flight #239 from Frankfurt at 4 pm. My orders listed "Jeffrey W. Lack/BMS" as the name to be used on my sign to find my passenger. He and his colleagues worked at the German Distribution Center of Bristol-Myers Squibb, and they were coming in to spend four days with their boss here at the Princeton-based international office.

On the passenger seat next to me lay my copy of the company's pickup orders, the signs I would hold up when picking up my passengers at the gate, and my trusty book of the Mercer County Streets. This book was my most valued tool when trying to pick up my customers at their homes because this was long before the GPS era. I had used my maps earlier this morning to find my first passenger's home at 4 am in the countryside between Princeton and Hopewell. Mr. Henry was ready and waiting and in a very good mood because his driver was on time. He told me he would request me as his driver from now on because he'd be able to relax when waiting, knowing I was punctual and dependable. He told me that several times the driver sent to pick him up wouldn't be able to find his home in the early morning darkness and when he finally arrived at the airport, he would barely make his plane in time. I promised him I'd try never to run late, assuring him he didn't have to worry any more. I dropped him off at Newark airport (EWR) at 5:30 am, giving him lots of time before his 7 am flight.

After dropping him off, I pulled into our Newark-Airport-Limo-Hangout located at the local McDonalds restaurant and drank several cups of coffee while reading three chapters of my newest copy of John Grisham's bestseller, *Pelican Brief*. One perk that comes with being a limousine driver is the vast amount of time to read in-between pickups, and I'd already read both of John Grisham's other books.

Soon it was time to head back to the airport and pick up my next passenger, Ms. Barbara Fleming. She would be arriving at the arrival platform of Terminal B soon after her flight landed, which was expected to arrive at 8:30 am. I parked the car and soon was inside, standing among a long line of limousine drivers (yes, all men), holding up my sign with her name on it. Soon, an attractive woman came down the escalator and scanned all the passenger signs until her eyes hit mine with her name in bold black letters.

"Hello, I'm Barbara," she said in a soft voice.

"Good morning. I'm Lois, your driver," I responded.

"What a nice surprise to finally have a lady driver. I've been using A-1 for years, but never had a woman greet me before," she remarked. I smiled as I took the carry-on luggage from her hand as she informed me it was the only luggage she brought on this trip. We were off to my car and soon on our way toward Canal Pointe in Princeton where she lived. While she made her phone calls to family and colleagues at her office, I headed straight to the driveway of her condo, thanks again to my trusty street-map book.

My next pickup at 11 am was my friend, Professor Frank von Hippel, at the Woodrow Wilson School of Public and International Politics at Princeton University. I parked and went inside to inform his secretary that I was there to pick the professor up and take him to the Princeton Junction train station to catch his Amtrak train arriving at 11:30. Right about then, the professor walked in.

"Good morning, Professor von Hippel. It's my pleasure to drive you to your train this morning," I said with a big smile. I really liked Frank so much. He was such a warm, gentle person, and so easy to talk with.

"Well, good morning Lois. How nice to have you escort me today. Tell me, how are all your friends in Kazakhstan these days?" he asked.

"I just spoke with Olzhas Suleimenov last week to confirm that his delegation arrived home safely. They certainly had a whirlwind trip through the United States two months ago, and I can't thank you enough for helping us with hosting some of them," I exclaimed. "May I take your luggage for you?" I asked.

"Absolutely not, Lois. You just lead the way to our car, thank you."

Once he was settled in my car, he told me he was on his way to meet with Bill Clinton and his advising committee as they prepared for the 1992 Democratic Convention coming up in July. Frank had written extensively on the technical basis for nuclear nonproliferation and disarmament initiatives and the future of nuclear energy. His book, *Citizen Scientist*, published less than a year ago, had caught the Clinton peoples' eye and they needed advice from this top American scientist. Little did Professor von Hippel know that one year later, during 1993 and 1994, he would serve under President Bill

Clinton as the Assistant Director for National Security in the White House Office of Science and Technology Policy.

Professor von Hippel waved goodbye from the train platform and I headed back to my office three miles away to use the restroom before heading out for my next long trip to JFK. It takes 1.5–2 hours on a good day to drive from Princeton to JFK, so I learned early in my training to give myself plenty of time when heading out to make a pickup. By leaving around noon, I should be there before two, providing this is one of those "good days." (A good day is one with no bad weather to affect flight schedules, and not too much traffic on the Belt Parkway. Otherwise you can sit an hour or two – or longer – in standing traffic.). The company had taught me how to call the airlines and confirm the up-to-date expected arrival time, so once I arrived in the arrival parking lot I called to confirm. If the flight was delayed a little, I'd stay in my car and read until it was time to land. Today is one of those "good days," so I only read one chapter of *Pelican Brief* before going inside the terminal.

The flight arrived at 4:15 pm and my passengers appeared through the Arrivals door after they passed through customs around 5 pm. I was standing with another fifty or more limo drivers, all men except me, holding our signs over our heads. Because my passengers had called the A-1 home office as soon as their airplane landed, they knew they would be looking for a lady driver in her fifties, so it took only one glance to find me.

Once we shook hands and I offered to help them with their luggage, we were off for my car. All three of my gentlemen passengers insisted on pulling their own suitcases, so I led them out into the parking lot like the mother duck leading her ducklings behind her. We soon found my shiny Cadillac glistening in the late afternoon sunshine. We were off in a flash and quickly entered the slow-moving line of five o'clock traffic on the Belt Parkway. The three colleagues talked among themselves for fifteen or twenty minutes and then asked me if I'd ever been to Germany. Wham! They opened my "window of opportunity" and I was off to entertain them for the next two hours.

"No, unfortunately I haven't visited Germany yet, except to change planes at the Frankfort airport. But I did spend a week in Prague, Czechoslovakia last August just before I took my delegation into the former Soviet Union for a two-week trip from Moscow, through Volgograd, down to Almaty, Kazakhstan and up to Pavlodor and Semipalatinsk," I answered.

Instantly, I could see in my rear-view mirror the shock on all three faces as they tried to absorb the fact that this middle-aged lady limo driver from NJ had traveled halfway around the world into the Republic of Kazakhstan, a foreign country even Europeans hadn't penetrated yet.

"You have been to Kazakhstan?" Mr. Lack exclaimed. "That is so exciting. Very few people in Germany are familiar with Kazakhstan yet. Whatever took you to such a remote region of the world?" So for more than an hour, I told them all about how I first met Olzhas Suleimenov, my friend from the Kremlin; why he asked me to bring a delegation of American citizens to visit his country; all about our trip to the Soviet Nuclear Test site in the desert outside Semipalatinsk; how the people of that region were suffering from the horrible symptoms of radiation disease following forty years of testing nuclear weapons; and the desperate need for medicines for the radiation victims. I explained that now, since the former Soviet Union has crumbled and each Republic was trying to survive the separation from Moscow and all the other Republics, there wasn't even aspirin to treat the pain for those suffering.

I answered dozens of their questions and then they all expressed their admiration for the citizen diplomacy work my organization and I were doing.

The BMS home office seemed to appear out of nowhere, and as I held the door open for my passengers to exit the car, each man shook my hand. Then Mr. Lack handed me his business card and said, "Lois, I want you to telephone our boss, Berry Wilson, who has his office right here in this building. I wrote his name and private telephone number on the back of my card. He is President of the European Division of BMS and I'm certain he would offer to help the people of Kazakhstan with their need for medicine."

"Thank you, Mr. Lack. I will give him a call," I said as the three men walked toward the gorgeous, immense BMS building.

That night when I arrived home, I taped the business card showing Berry Wilson's name on the wall behind my desk directly over my telephone. I had every intention of calling him – when the time was right!

For the next four months I worked twelve hours a day, six days a week and soon I recovered financially from my recent twenty-eight-day excursion around the USA. I paid Barbara back the $2,000 it cost to rent the van that I drove my Kazakh delegation in back in April – and paid off my big telephone bill. I was finally free of any financial burden, but as my life would dictate, that freedom didn't last very long.

During those previous four months, I had numerous encounters with other BMS employees traveling to and from the German Distribution Center to the home office in Princeton. Again, I had that two-hour window while driving from JFK to their destination to tell them all about Kazakhstan, and their interest soon made it apparent that they had already heard of my experiences and wanted to confirm the stories for themselves. Every one of them exited my car with the same advice – "Talk to our boss, Berry Wilson."

Finally, on a cold and rainy October 2, four months after first meeting Mr. Lack and hanging up his business card on my office wall, I was working at my desk when I heard a fax starting to come through on my fax machine. I stood over the fax machine as it slowly spit out its document. It was very seldom that I had a fax come through, so I got all excited and stood over the machine, trying to read the message as it was being printed. When it was done printing, I sat in amazement and shock. Could I possibly believe my eyes? Was I hallucinating? How could this possibly be? I must have read it over a dozen times before I moved one inch from my chair.

Dear Ms. Nikolai,

I wish to invite you and your World Citizen Diplomat delegation to attend our First Annual TV-Marathon Auction to raise money to build a children's hospital here in Alma Ata for our children suffering from radiation disease resulting from the nuclear testing at the Semipalatinsk Nuclear Test site. It will be held on Saturday, October 17, 1992 and I will personally serve as the Grand Chairwoman of the event. All of us here in Kazakhstan hope you will attend. Please respond as soon as possible.

Yours in Friendship,

Sara Nazarbayeva

First Lady of Kazakhstan

The first thing I thought was maybe one of my friends decided to play a really cruel joke by sending me this fax. I just imagined they were sick of hearing me describe our experiences last September when we were flown up to the desert near Semipalatinsk and celebrated the closing of the Soviet nuclear test site with all the Kazakh citizens, so they decided to pull this trick on me. But when I looked at the fax more closely, I realized it had been sent from a foreign phone number.

Then I tried to figure out how the First Lady ever found out my name, phone, and fax numbers. That was when I remembered what Umyt and Zhamil had told me recently by telephone, that they had seen a documentary on National Kazakh television showing the closing of the test site. It was recorded the day we were up there, and the name of the documentary was *American Grandmother Brings U.S. Delegation to Help Celebrate Closing Soviet Nuclear Test Site.* Umyt said it must have been shown a hundred times over the past year. Zhamil said they probably did that to help the average Kazakh people lose their fear of Americans and democracy – the two things they had been schooled to fear over the past seventy years of Cold War between our two nations. I remembered giving my business card to the young man with the microphone that day who was putting the film together. He must have given my card to the First Lady.

As I was sitting at my desk in disbelief, I happened to look up and right there – as big as life – was the card Mr. Lack gave me with Berry Wilson's name and office telephone number printed in large letters staring right back at me. For the past four months I never felt comfortable calling him, and now today seemed like the perfect opportunity to give him a call. Maybe they would send over some medicine or money with me to present at this TV-Marathon Auction. And maybe they would even pay my flight to attend? I decided it was worth a try to at least call him and let him know about the invitation.

"Hello, this is Lois Nicolai calling. I live here in Princeton and Mr. Jeffrey Lack from the BMS German Distribution Center recommended I call to speak with Mr. Berry Wilson about my contacts in Kazakhstan. Would he happen to be in this late in the day?" I asked.

"Just one moment, Ms. Nicolai. I will check to see if he is still here," his secretary responded.

A good two minutes passed by while I was having crazy ideas go through my head. Could he possibly already have a file on me with everything I had told Mr. Lack and all the other employees? Then I realized these are the kind of thoughts that go through a person's mind when she reads too many John Grisham books! Right about the time I cleared my head, a voice came on the line.

"Hello Ms. Nicolai. This is Berry Wilson. I've been looking forward to hearing from you. Several of my colleagues from Germany have told me some great stories that you shared with them on their rides to and from JFK. Please tell me why you are kind enough to call me today," he said.

For the next ten or fifteen minutes I summarized the situation in Kazakhstan, concluding with the fact that they had absolutely no medicine in the entire country, not even aspirin. Then I told him about the fax invitation I just received from the First Lady of Kazakhstan, Sara Nazarbayeva herself. I told him I would be happy to take a gift from Bristol-Myers Squibb, if he chose to send one.

"Ms. Nicolai, I am leaving tomorrow afternoon for our European office in Germany. Could you possibly put a written request together that I could take with me, and bring it here to my office before noon? Is this possible? Since this fundraiser is coming up in just fifteen days, I will have to move very quickly to try to make any kind of contribution," Mr. Wilson explained.

"Absolutely! I'll have it in your secretary's hand by noon tomorrow. Thank you very much for considering my request," I said as we ended our conversation.

Oh my God! How will I prepare a professional request and have it in Berry Wilson's hands in less than 24 hours? I thought out loud. But that thought lasted only a second, because I knew I had to make this happen.

I pulled out the file I had in my desk with the list of medicines Olzhas Suleimenov gave me last year. I decided to go to Kinko's on Spring Street to put my proposal together. I used one of their computers – at $10 an hour – and then bound it into a professional presentation. Kinko's was open all night. Remember, Princeton is a university town, and from what I had observed while living there, students seem to do their best studying in the middle of the night. I arrived at 7 pm and worked until midnight putting a complete information packet together. I had it bound with a clear plastic front cover. I put the cover letter on our World Citizen Diplomat (WCD) stationary, and it stood out beautifully under the clear plastic. The completed packet looked great to me and I had the two employees proofread it to be certain it was in good form. It was in Berry Wilson's secretary's hands at 11 am the next morning.

One week later, on Monday, October 12, I received a four-page fax from Jeffrey W. Lack in Germany informing me that Bristol-Myers Squibb was pleased to donate two very precious products to the children in Kazakhstan suffering from refractory childhood acute lymphoblastic leukemia. The first drug, Vm-26 (Teniposide) was to be used in combination with other anti-cancer drugs. The second was Isocal, a nutritionally complete formula for tube and oral feeding in post-operative and cancer patients. The value of the donation at market prices was $60,000.

Mr. Lack explained in the fax that they couldn't have the items available in such short time, so they enclosed an official letter to the First Lady guaranteeing the donation, and suggested the letter be used during the ceremony. BMS also requested shipping instructions and the names of the people in Alma Ata who would guarantee delivery to the intended recipients. Mr. Lack also requested that we meet with him and his secretary, Ms. Margret Pfeuffer, in Moscow on our way down to Alma Ata for the ceremony. Unfortunately, BMS didn't offer to pay for my flight, but how could I complain when they had come through with such a fantastic gift for the children of Kazakhstan!

I was so excited that I could hardly keep from shouting with joy! What an unbelievable honor to be able to present this generous gift to the First Lady. The first thing I did was call twenty members of WCD and asked each of them if they would like to accompany me to Kazakhstan in five days to attend the first TV-Marathon Auction in Alma Ata. As much as everyone wished they could go, five days just wasn't enough time for them to get off work. This didn't present a problem for me because when I was hired at A-1, I had explained to Mr. Starr how I was actively involved in peace and international relations projects that occasionally took me on short-term trips throughout the world. He agreed to hire me with the understanding that I could return to my same 3 am position whenever I returned from these missions.

Fortunately, my friend, Shariffa Khan, was able to make arrangements in such short notice, and the two of us immediately began our preparations to leave in five days.

On Tuesday, October 13, Shariffa and I drove down to the Kazakh Embassy in Washington D.C. to apply for our visas. We dropped off our passports and the invitation letter at 11 am, went to lunch and arrived back at the embassy at 2 pm where we found the passports ready to go. Of course, it did help a whole lot to have a letter of invitation from the First Lady of Kazakhstan herself! Visas usually are not issued nearly that easy. I knew because I had lots of experience when taking my groups abroad the past few years.

That evening I called Pan Am Airlines and made reservations for the two of us to fly out on Thursday. Thank God I had Wednesday to pick up the necessities I needed for the trip, pack, contact all my children, and close up my apartment before we left in the middle of the night for an early morning flight. We arrived in Moscow in the early afternoon, eight hours after departing from JFK in New York, and quickly made our way to the hotel where we were to meet Mr. Lack and Ms. Pfeuffer. There we discussed the presentation coming up in Alma Ata and the need to solidify delivery arrangements. The last thing he wanted was for the medicine to accidentally end up in black market hands.

On Friday morning we flew down to Alma Ata on Aeroflot Airlines, arriving before noon. We were met at the airport by our friends Umyt and Zhamil, and they took us straight back to their flat to unpack and relax before the big day. Umyt loved to cook, so she had a wonderful Kazakh meal in front of us early that evening and we hit the bed before ten. The next day was surely going to be a big day for all of us.

To Be Continued . . .

Jeffrey W. Lack
General Manager
Commonwealth of Independent States

9 October 1992

Ms. Lois Nicolai
World Citzien Diplomats
P.O. Box 1484
Princeton, NJ 08542
USA

Dear Ms. Nicolai,

We are pleased to inform you that Bristol-Myers Squibb will donate to the children of Kazakhstan, through your organization, the following products which we believe could be of real importance:

1. Vm-26 (Teniposide), indicated in combination with other anticancer drugs, for patients with refractory childhood acute lymphoblastic leukaemia.

2. Isocal (nutritionally complete formula) for tube and oral feeding in post-operative and cancer patients.

The value of the donation at market prices is of $60,000. Unfortunately, it is not possible to have the items available in the short time required. I am herewith enclosing a letter guaranteeing the donation which you may use during the ceremony.

Additionally, we will need precise shipping instructions and name of people in Alma Ata who will guarantee delivery to the intended recipients.

BRISTOL-MYERS SQUIBB GMBH, Volkartstraße 83, D-8000 München 19
Telefon (089) 13 03-0, Telex 5 23 719, Telefax (089) 130 33 92, Teletex 897 105 = BMSMuen, Telegramm: BMS München
Dresdner Bank AG München, Konto 3 017 461, BLZ 700 800 00, Postgiroamt München, Konto 402 75-801, BLZ 700 100 80

- 2 -

Finally, as I explained over the phone, I would welcome the opportunity for one of the members of our staff in Moscow or our representative in Alma Ata to be present at the donation. For this I would kindly require your detailed schedule and hotel in Alma Ata for us to be in contact with yourself during your trip. I will personally be in Moscow next week where I can be reached at

> BMS- Moscow Office
> 1-Krasnogvardeisky pr. 25 b
> 123100 Moscow
>
> Tel.: 95-25 64 044
> Fax: 95-25 39 784

Your itinerary should be also sent to our Munich office (fax number 89-12142-467).

Sincerely,

Jeffrey W. Lack

CHAPTER 10 – PART 2

AN UNEXPECTED INVITATION FROM A VERY FAMOUS LADY

Saturday morning, Umyt and Zhamil escorted Shariffa and me to the superb Soviet-style Performing Arts building where all the daily activities were already in progress. The daytime hours were set aside to honor and entertain all the children. There were thousands of families roaming the grounds. It had rained during the night before, so puddles still shined beneath the entertainer's feet. But by no means did the wet pavement dampen all the excitement surrounding the building.

As we walked toward the main stairway in front of the building, we passed many tables displaying homemade cookies and candies for sale. It was amazing that they looked so much like our American delicacies. Then came the rows of all kinds of cakes, pies and other pastries. Of course, we had to try some, and they were delicious.

When we approached the top stair, we saw a huge swing on the left side of the building with four young Kazakh teenage girls riding it. They were in their dazzling national floor-length dresses of pink, burgundy, and gold. Because it was very damp and cold, they all had coats on, but their dresses stood out beautifully.

Under the main sign announcing the ceremony, which was hanging over the center of the building, was a marvelous-sounding musical orchestra. There were at least two dozen men and women, all in various national attire, playing their Kazakh instruments and producing some of the most bewitching music. As soon as I heard their music, my memories of the previous year in the desert of Semipalatinsk came alive. I was once again spellbound by the people and customs of this exotic, exciting culture.

My attention was jolted back to the present when I saw ten-foot human puppet people walking around on the stage. They were mesmerizing. They had both male and female faces, probably made of papier-mâché. Their clothing was absolutely unique, and they stood several feet taller than even Zhamil, who was six foot three. Now that I have seen *Avatar*, they compared to them in size, but they looked more like ten-foot tall dolls. They were simply extraordinary.

Umyt, Zhamil, Shariffa, and I walked around the area of festivities for at least three hours, applauding at the various musical events, smiling at the children and shaking hands with hundreds of their parents. Shariffa and I stood out like a vanilla and chocolate popsicle – me with my white skin and big round eyes and Shariffa with her shiny Zimbabwean-African brown skin. Most of the Kazakh people have black hair, light to olive complexions and slanted eyes. Everyone there knew we were strangers from afar.

Shariffa loved the giant swings and soon ventured up to talk with the girls taking turns swinging. As I looked up at her, I was impressed by her charisma and charm. Her warm, friendly smile brought happiness to everyone around her. Shariffa was born in

Zimbabwe and received her secondary schooling there. When she was in her twenties, she informed her family that she intended to travel to America. She arrived in the USA in 1964 and found work as a veterinarian assistant in Trenton, New Jersey. In her late twenties, she decided to go back to school and eventually earned both her bachelor and master's degrees, allowing her to qualify for a position with the Trenton Prison system. She soon settled in Bordentown and worked for the Department of Juvenile Corrections for the past two decades, helping young people put their lives back together.

Shariffa joined our World Citizen Diplomats (WCD) group in Princeton in early 1991 and instantly became an active member. Her love of travel and international background attracted her to us and vice versa. She stood out at all our social events in her colorful print Zimbabwean dresses and unique Gahanna head wraps. I was so thrilled she could join me on this important trip.

Around three o'clock in the afternoon, our friends led us to their car and insisted we go back to their apartment to freshen up and rest before the evening event.

"But Umyt, I thought this 'was' the event. Is there more this evening?" I asked.

"Oh yes, Lois. This is just the children's festivities. Tonight, there will be a program inside the performing arts building for all those adults who have paid a heavy price for tickets. There will be some entertainment by various professional Kazakh and Russian entertainers; there will be speeches by several government officials who helped in some way to support the event; and there will be many large donations made by various rich Kazakhs who will also speak as they drop their rubles into the large flask on the stage. It is a dressy affair, so you'll see how the rich and famous of our country present themselves," Umyt exclaimed as Zhamil translated.

"Oh dear, Umyt, I hope the dressy outfit I brought with me is suitable. I don't want to be too underdressed."

"Lois," Umyt said, "whatever you and Shariffa wear will be more than acceptable. Once the audience hears your name and then what you brought with you, they will be so excited. Your outfit will mean nothing to them. Remember what Olzhas told us last year? He told you, in our presence, that you are a 'legend in your own time' here in Kazakhstan for celebrating the closing of the test site with our people. To my people you are a real, living, and breathing hero."

I did remember what Olzhas said. In fact, I have never been able to quite grasp his remark. Whenever I think about it, I feel so honored and so proud, but it doesn't actually seem real. I often think back on that remarkable day celebrating with thousands of Kazakhs in the desert sand outside Semipalatinsk – it all seems like a fairytale that I must have dreamt. And now here I am, one year later, as the personal guest of the First Lady of Kazakhstan herself. And to top it all off, Bristol-Myers Squibb had been gracious enough to provide us with a generous gift of medicine to present tonight at this first TV-Marathon auction. How could I ever be so lucky? Me – just an ordinary, average, middle-aged grandmother who never had an extra penny in her pocket and yet, as poor as I am, I love every day of my life. How can this be possible?

Umyt broke my train of thought by calling us to her luscious dinner table to enjoy her delicious stuffed peppers and all the trimmings of another scrumptious meal. We had a chance to rest a good hour before we dressed for our evening affair. Thank goodness I had packed my black sequined blouse and silk black skirt, just in case there was a dressy occasion. Our driver was there to pick us up at 7:30 pm sharp, and we arrived at the Kazakh Performing Arts building by quarter to eight – early enough to enter the building with the masses of people.

"Oh my, Umyt, how gorgeous everyone looks tonight. Your Kazakh national dresses that so many ladies are wearing are absolutely breathtaking, so bright and colorful. And those young women not in national attire look like they are all wearing French creations that were personally fitted for them in Paris," I exclaimed.

"Is it possible that they were personally fitted in Paris?" Shariffa inquired.

"Yes, Shariffa," Umyt responded through Zhamil's translation, "many of those here tonight are the rich and famous of Kazakhstan who now live abroad in Europe, Dubai, and in America. But they all came back to their beloved Kazakhstan this weekend to attend our first TV-Marathon auction to donate big contributions to benefit the children suffering from radiation disease,"

"This is the first big event we have celebrated since our president declared independence from the Soviet Union last year. Our citizens are so excited and proud to have survived the break without any bloodshed. This is a true night of celebration for us here in Almaty," Zhamil added.

"I didn't realize how important this event is to all your people, Zhamil," I said. "I was just excited about the possibility of a new hospital to care for all the very sick children suffering from radiation caused by the nuclear testing. Now I understand that this event is so much more important, since it represents the building of your new nation from the citizen level up. Shariffa and I are so fortunate to be here today."

The children's daytime activities had ended, and all the families had returned to their homes. I was amazed to see that the front of the building, as well as the staircase leading to the entrance, had been cleared off of the musicians, dancers, and puppets present earlier, and colorfully dressed women and men were now ascending upon this lovely building highlighted by the spotlights shining from every direction.

Once inside the lobby we quickly felt the warmth of the crowd, although experiencing a huge cultural shock. The hundreds of Kazakh citizens were dressed in sumptuous, exotic Kazakh finery, both men and women alike. They were wearing many varieties of their traditional Kazakh costumes that have withstood the test of time in beauty and style, which is why they are still worn today to honor their ancient fashion. Their traditional costumes are designed and tailored from valuable plush, velvet, crape, satin, silk, brocade, and other expensive fabrics. To make them more sophisticated, these clothes were artistically embroidered with gold and silver threads and decorated with pearls, corals, and carnelian insertions. The most beautiful dresses were those with delicate silk fringes. These dresses are referred to as *koilek*, and the ladies looked very graceful in their long dresses. *Kunikey koilek* is made of light, fluffy material densely gathered at the waist. The long sleeves are also gathered. These dresses make the women seem like enigmatic fairy beauties, literally "sun-like," as in the meaning of the Kazakh word *kunikey*!

The traditional man's wear consists of the famous headgear called his *borik*. He wears a suede coat, called the *zhargak shapan*. His decorative belt is a *beldik*. His suede trousers are *zhargak shalbar*, and his high boots are made from suede also.

The mixture of Russian and Kazakh languages was mesmerizing, and the magnificent exotic Kazakh music, led by the Kazakh *dombra*, was exhilarating. Music was very special in the life of their nomadic ancestors, with many myths and legends throughout their Kazakh folklore. Their most popular instrument is the *dombra*, a two-stringed instrument with an oval, or rarely, a triangle body. The strings are made from twisted sheep's intestines. It can be played sitting, standing, or on horseback.

Another ancient musical instrument still used today is the *zhetygen*, consisting of seven strings. The legend behind this instrument tells how the sacred figure "seven" is a symbol of life, and the belief is that the vibrations from this instrument generates a new life cycle.

Still another favorite instrument is the *kobyz*, which represents the balance between the courses of life and death on Earth. This is a bowed instrument with a concave neck and a big-dipper-like body with an open upper side. The strings and bow are made of horsehair. Their favorite wind instrument is the *sybyzgy*, shaped like a longitudinal flute.

"Shariffa, can you believe this is such an extravaganza?" I asked.

"This is so much more than I ever imagined it would be. What a shame all our members could not have come with us," Shariffa responded.

Right about then, the lights flickered and Umyt grabbed my arm. "It's time for us to go in and take our seats," Umyt said. Shariffa and I followed Umyt and Zhamil into the elegant auditorium.

To Be Continued . . .

1992

LEFT TO RIGHT: Young teenage Kazakh ladies standing with their large swings along with Lois, Shariffa and Umyt at the national celebration for building the first children's hospital in Almaty for those suffering from acute leukemia brought on by the nuclear testing in the Semipalatinsk Region of Kazakhstan.

Lovely lady dancers performing to beautiful exotic Kazakh music

These were ten-foot-tall puppets that left you mesmerized
and spellbound.

The daytime celebration was specifically for the children.

The display of fresh fruits and tasty pastries was bountiful and enticing.

A few of the Kazakh musical instruments and a group of children in their national Kazakh attire.

TOP: Zhamil, Umyt, Lois, First Lady Sarah Nazarbaeva, Shariffa, and Mrs. Nazarbaeva's private secretary in the office of the First Lady of Kazakhstan. BOTTOM: Umyt, Lois, Secretary of Transportation for Kazakhstan, Zhamil, Shariffa and Secretary of Transportation of Kergystan.

CHAPTER 11 – PART 3

AN UNEXPECTED INVITATION FROM A VERY FAMOUS LADY

Shariffa and I followed Umyt and Zhamil inside the theater. The chandeliers glistened, accentuating the silvery and light blue star-studded ceiling. The lovely usherette smiled when Zhamil explained who we were, and the four of us were led down the main aisle to the third row from the stage. The young lady explained to Zhamil that our seats were the third through the sixth in the middle of the third row, directly in front of the gigantic stage. The chairs were upholstered in light sea-blue velvet, lined around the edges with dark blue satin. It was the most elegant and comfortable chair I ever sat in. The usherette soon seated two large men on each side of us, whom Zhamil informed me were Kazakh secret service undercover agents.

We sat back and relaxed as we observed a small group of musicians warming up their exotic Kazakh dombra strings and sybyzgy flutes. Just before the lights were lowered, the First Lady, Sara Nazarbaeva, entered from the left corner of the stage and walked down to the first row of seats with her entourage of bodyguards and associates. She then blew a kiss to Shariffa and me before sitting down two rows in front of us.

Soon, the lights were dimmed and the festivities began. For two solid hours many famous Russian, Kirgizia, and Kazakh singers sang; ballads and folksongs, accompanied by musical instrumentalists, were played; clowns frolicked throughout the audience; and numerous citizens were introduced as they mounted the stage to drop their rubles into the gigantic flask at our far right. Each donor was allowed to give a short speech.

Around 9:15 pm the bright chandelier lights were lit and I assumed we would now enjoy the half-time intermission. Suddenly the door on the left of the stage opened and this time President Nazarbayev entered into the auditorium. He waved to all as he walked down to the first row of chairs and joined the First Lady, two rows directly in front of us. There had not been anyone seated in the second row, so it felt like we could reach out and touch both their shoulders if we chose. I looked over at Zhamil and asked if we would be able to go out into the lobby for something to drink because I had begun to feel nervous and thirsty. However, as I looked around the theater, no one seemed to be moving from their seats. Zhamil just smiled at me, and then the young usherette appeared in the aisle next to our row. The Master of Ceremonies walked to the center of the stage and began speaking in Russian. Of course, I didn't know what he was saying until I heard Bristol-Myers Squibb mentioned, and then both Shariffa's and my name. The audience stood clapping, and Zhamil grabbed my arm and led me out of our aisle and up to the front of the auditorium. As the audience took their seats, Zhamil led me not more than two feet from the President and First Lady. He whispered in my ear that the usherette instructed me to not speak too long.

Oh my God, I was about to address the President and First Lady of Kazakhstan – and more than a thousand of the most prominent citizens in their new country! As I looked in front of me, I saw the President scooting forward in his chair and staring straight into my eyes. I remember how quiet the entire auditorium became as I gasped for the air I needed to make my words audible. Thank God I had experience throughout my life speaking in public, but even with all that experience it took a lot to force those first words to come out. Once I started speaking though, my words began to flow somewhat easily. As I spoke, Zhamil translated for the audience in Russian.

Good Evening President Nazarbayev, First Lady Nazarbayeva and citizens of this exciting new nation of Kazakhstan. It is Shariffa's and my pleasure this evening to present a gift of medicine from Bristol-Myers Squibb Pharmaceutical Company to the children suffering from radiation diseases resulting from the nuclear testing in Semipalatinsk.

As you know, members of my World Citizen Diplomats organization from Princeton, New Jersey, accompanied me to your closing of the nuclear test site last September, and we now understand the terrible health hazards those forty years of testing brought to your nation.

The officials at Bristol-Myers Squibb hope this medicine will help save the lives of many children who are the victims. Thank you all for making us feel welcome today and tonight, and I pray your new hospital will be built quickly to accommodate all the children who need the life-saving care. Peace and love to all of you.

I shook hands with both the President and the First Lady as the hundreds of citizens in attendance jumped to their feet again. Never in my entire life did I ever have a standing ovation before. My heart almost jumped out of my body as Zhamil led me back to my seat while the entire audience cheered. I flopped down in that lavish velvet chair overwhelmed. I could not believe such an event was happening, and I saw the same expression of incredulity on Shariffa's face. It took me a long time to be able to breathe normally again. What a remarkable experience for two ordinary citizens to have!

Now it was the "real" intermission. The four of us needed a quick vodka to calm our nerves, plus restrooms were badly in demand. A few minutes later, the lights flickered to signal us back to our seats. We then enjoyed another two hours of entertainment. Many more citizens were introduced as they approached the stage and dropped their rubles into the big glass flask, each giving their sixty-second speech of a lifetime. It was such a transporting experience that I honestly cannot remember our drive home that evening. But I do remember lying in bed later that night still bubbling with excitement, reliving an evening we would not have imagined.

Once I fell asleep, I slept like a baby. I remember waking up feeling especially refreshed and rested. It was the first really good night's sleep I'd had in the past two weeks of frantic preparations and traveling halfway around the world.

As I entered Umyt's fragrant kitchen, I saw a meal fit for a king spread out on her table. "Oh Umyt, you have prepared such a beautiful breakfast. I'm famished! I see everyone is up ahead of me. Sorry! I hope I didn't hold you all back from enjoying your breakfast."

"It is perfectly fine, Lois, and we hope you had a good night's sleep," Zhamil said. Since Umyt spoke only a little English, Zhamil was our spokesperson. "Umyt wants you to know that we already received a telephone call this morning – and it was from the First Lady's office."

"Oh, how exciting. I hope she was satisfied with my little speech last night. I hope she didn't feel it was too long."

"Not only was she impressed with your presentation, but she had her secretary call to invite you to meet with her at her private office tomorrow to discuss the shipment of medicine," Zhamil continued.

"How fantastic! Shariffa, did you hear this? We're going to meet with the First Lady personally. This trip just keeps getting more and more exciting. When does she want us there, Zhamil?"

"We agreed to be at her office in the Presidential Palace at 2:00 tomorrow afternoon. I hope this is okay with you, Lois?"

"Absolutely," I gasped.

We all sat down to enjoy Umyt's spread of delicious foods: fried eggs, two kinds of homemade breads, sausages and salami, cottage cheese, yogurt, fresh fruits, pancakes, coffee, and tea. The eggs were fried harder than I normally prefer, because I like a runny yolk, but Zhamil told us that Umyt is very careful to cook everything extremely well done so no one gets salmonella. He said salmonella is a big problem in Almaty. She also boiled the water before scrubbing vegetables and fruits, so we wouldn't get diarrhea or an upset stomach. Umyt was the perfect hostess, which I already knew from my previous trips to Kazakhstan, and she always took the best possible care of us.

This whole weekend was as important for Umyt and Zhamil as it was exciting for Shariffa and me. Umyt was an important businesswoman in Almaty, and this meeting would open many new doors for her, business wise. She had hopes of opening the first pharmaceutical factory in Kazakhstan, and her opportunity to meet the First Lady would be beneficial to her.

As soon as we all finished breakfast and lingered over our second cups of coffee, Zhamil informed us that he and Umyt would like to take us to the most famous spot in Almaty today – Medeo!

As soon as Umyt's kitchen was clean and shiny again we were picked up by their private driver, Amantai. Neither Umyt nor Zhamil drove, so they relied on Amantai to drive them wherever they went. They weren't his only employer, so Zhamil would call Amantai at his private home and reserve him whenever they needed a ride. Amantai drove a lovely black Mercedes sedan and was both handsome and professional. Over the many years that he drove for Umyt and Zhamil, he had become a very close and trusted friend.

Zhamil instructed him to take the four of us up to Medeu, a beautiful mountain valley located thirteen kilometers from the center of Almaty, on the south-eastern outskirts of the city. Zhamil told us that among the peaceful nature and other attractions of this valley is Medeo, which was the world's largest speed skating rink in the 70s and 80s. It sits 1,691 meters above sea level, making it also the highest skating rink in the world. It has 10,000 square meters of ice and utilizes a sophisticated freezing and watering system to ensure the ice quality.

South of the skating rink is Medeu Dam, built to protect both the rink and the city of Almaty itself from potentially devastating mud slides.

Umyt informed Zhamil in Russian to tell us that after the collapse of the Soviet Union last year, the costs to uphold the arena as a top rink proved too expensive for the newly independent Republic of Kazakhstan, so now the future of Medeo was becoming very uncertain.

Zhamil said, "The Men's World Speed Skating Championship in 1988 was the last great competition held at Medeo, and it was won by the American skater Eric Flaim."

Our trip to the top of the dam was interesting on this gorgeous, clear fall day, and our afternoon excursion began and ended perfectly.

Early the next morning, the sun peaked over the mountain-top high above Almaty. All four of us were up bright and early, too excited to sleep knowing we would soon meet with the First Lady. At breakfast, we discussed our strategy for the afternoon meeting. I had already prepared notes of what I wanted to discuss, and Umyt asked Zhamil to translate while she shared her suggestions. Soon we had our agenda pretty much outlined and we all scattered throughout their small four-room flat to take some quiet time to ourselves as we personally prepared for this important meeting.

Amantai arrived to pick up the four of us and we arrived at the Presidential Palace at 1:30 pm. We were escorted to the waiting room outside the First Lady's office where we sat, practically holding our breath in silence, until the door to her office opened. The First Lady's secretary entered and greeted us before he escorted our little group in to meet the First Lady. He was a man probably in his late fifties who had a very professional appearance. He wore a gray suit with a burgundy print tie and a soft light blue shirt. His hair was short and nicely styled. He appeared very westernized. Unfortunately, we never recorded his name and never learned anything about his personal life. He did not speak English, so all his communication was directed to Zhamil and Umyt.

I assumed the First Lady was in her early fifties, because I knew the President was fifty-two years old, three years younger than me. She wore a nicely tailored black wool suit, with a soft pale green silk blouse and long, dangling white pearl earrings. Her thick black shoulder-length hair accentuated her full smiling, matronly face, and her typical squinty Kazakh eyes were warm and friendly.

We all shook hands and the First Lady motioned for us to sit with her at the conference table located in the center of the room. I noticed her private desk located at one corner of the office and it made me immediately relax to realize she chose to sit around the same table as the rest of us instead of behind her desk. It felt like she was offering us a gesture of respect and equality, instead of showing off her status as the First Lady. One wall was covered with brown paneling and the other three walls were painted the same shade of green as her blouse, suggesting to me that this soft green was one of her favorite colors. Since light green is known to be soothing and calming, it didn't surprise me that we all seemed to find it easy to relax with this lovely lady.

Because of the language barrier, the four of us had agreed earlier that Umyt would be the spokesperson and Zhamil would do all the translating. Kazakhstan was one of the fifteen Soviet Republics of the former USSR for the past seventy years. Russian was the only language allowed to be taught in Soviet schools for all those years, even though every republic had its own national language. Because Russian was taught in all the schools, the Kazakh language was only kept alive within the family structure until two years earlier when President Nazarbayev was elected and he ordered all Kazakh schools to teach both languages, Kazakh and Russian. Umyt was born into a Kazakh family and consequently she learned both languages because her parents spoke Kazakh and she was taught Russian in school. However, Zhamil was the son of a military Russian soldier and he only spoke Russian up until he entered his university days when he chose to learn English. Consequently, all his translations were Russian to English and vice versa.

Translations are very time consuming, so during our one-hour meeting, we probably accomplished only twenty-five to thirty minutes of actual discussion. To begin our dialogue, the First Lady asked me all about my family and life in the United States. I told her all about my six children and grandchildren, and that I was now utilizing the second half of my life to help bring understanding between the former Soviet citizens and our American people. She told me she had three daughters and that she graduated from university as an economics engineer before she married the president. She had recently founded and was now chair of the Bobek International Children's charity, created to help mothers and children, mostly by assisting them within the healthcare system. This was the organization that sponsored this magnificent event we attended two days ago. Shariffa also shared a highlight of her life both in Zimbabwe and in the United States.

Our first topic of discussion was to work out the delivery arrangements for the medicine, which was first and foremost on all our minds. Jeffrey Lack of Bristol-Myers Squibb had instructed me back in Moscow exactly how he wanted this to be done, so I presented the First Lady with his written suggestions, which he had prepared in Russian. She and her secretary, whom I soon realized was also her advisor, reviewed the instructions and they both agreed that everything was in excellent order.

Next, we explored other ways we could initiate exchanges between our two countries. It was agreed for us to bring an American representative of an adoption agency to develop communication with their many needy orphanages. We also agreed to bring a medical expert in dialysis to start an exchange between our local hospital and their hospital which specializes in dialysis. Umyt also had a window of opportunity to share a little of what she was tackling as a businesswoman, although I never asked her to explain what they discussed in detail.

Our hour with the First Lady seemed to end as abruptly as it began, but thank goodness, I did remember to ask her if we could have a picture taken together. Every time I look at that picture, I laugh when I observe Zhamil. This brilliant man who never spoke one word of English with an English-speaking person before we arrived last year for our three-week trip up to the nuclear test site, now speaks perfect English and translated for the First Lady of his nation. He studied English during his eight years of university education while majoring in philosophy and immunology, never once conversing with anyone except his Kazakh professor – who also never held a live conversation with an English-speaking person. This wonderfully gentle friend went to meet *his* First Lady at the Presidential Palace *in jeans and a sweater*. I do not see this as disrespectful. To me, he is a man of great character who refuses to be anyone except who he really is in his heart and soul. He is never out to impress anyone!

Our ride back to their flat that afternoon was exhilarating – knowing we all accomplished what we intended. I remember our five-hour flight back to Moscow on Aeroflot and our eight-hour flight on Pan Am from Moscow home. We couldn't talk enough about our experience halfway around the world. It was a trip almost too good to be true!

BRISTOL-MYERS SQUIBB

Der Gesundheit verpflichtet

BRISTOL-MYERS SQUIBB GMBH, Volkartstraße 83, D-8000 München 19

9 October 1992

TO WHOM IT MAY CONCERN

This is to confirm that Bristol-Myers Squibb will arrange through
the World Citizen Diplomats Association a donation of **$ 60,000**
for the children of Kazakhstan, consisting of 2500 cans of
Isocal, nutritional formula for cancer patients, and 500 pack of
VM-26 (Teniposide), indicated for patients with refractory
childhood acute lymphoblastic leukaemia.

Sincerely,

Jeffrey W. Lack
General Manager CIS

BRISTOL-MYERS SQUIBB GMBH, Volkartstraße 83, D-8000 München 19
Telefon (089) 1303-0, Telex 523719, Telefax (089) 1303392, Teletex 897105 / BMSMuen, Telegramm BMS München
Dresdner Bank AG München, Konto 3017461, BLZ 700 80000, Postgiroamt München, Konto 402 75-801, BLZ 700 100 80

BRISTOL-MYERS SQUIBB

TELEFAX

Telefax Nummer: Telefax Number:	001-609-921-1647
An: To:	Mrs Lois A. Nicolai
Kopie an: Copy to:	
Von: From:	Margret Pfeuffer Secretary to Jeffrey W. Lack
Direkte Faxnummer: Direct Fax Number:	(89)12142-467 Telefon Durchwahl: Direct Phone Number: (89)12142-235
Datum: Date:	22 December 1992 Seitenzahl inkl. Deckblatt: Pages incl. Cover Sheet:

Nachricht:
Message:

DONATION TO KAZAKHSTAN

Dear Mrs Nicolai,

please find below the requested shipment details for
Alma Ata:

    VUMON: 13 December 1992 on LH 3320
                     arrived on 14 Dec. 5:50 am
                     AWB 220-28927356

    ISOCAL: 2 December 1992 on LH 3320
                     arrived same day 5:50 pm
                     AWB 220-72391325

We do not know who accepted it, but our Moscow
office advised us that the shipments have arrived
safely.

The food supplement has to be administered orally,
so that no equipment will be necessary.

Wishing you a Merry Christmas and a Happy New Year,
I remain with best regards,

Margret Pfeuffer

BRISTOL-MYERS SQUIBB GMBH, Volkartstraße 83, D-8000 München 19
Telefon (089) 10 0 0, Telex 529 719, Telefax (089) 100 00 91
Teletex 897105=BMSMuen, Telegramm BMS München

CHAPTER 12

ESSAYS FROM INFLUENTIAL AND KNOWLEDGEABLE WORLD CITIZENS

REVEREND BERNARDITO C. AUZA

HELEN CALDICOTT

PAUL K. CHAPPELL

LINDA PENTZ-GUNTER

RICHARD FALK

REBECCA JOHNSON

JONATHAN GRANOFF

CYNTHIA LAZAROFF

FRANK VON HIPPEL

ALICE SLATER

KARIPBEK KUYUKOV

ARCHBISHOP BERNARDITO CLEOPAS AUZA

The Most Reverend Bernardito Auza, Apostolic Nuncio, is the Permanent Observer of the Holy See to the United Nations.

Archbishop Auza was born in Talibon, Philippines. He is the eighth of twelve children. He was ordained as a priest in June 1985.

In May 2008 he was appointed Titular Archbishop of Suacia, Montenegro, and Apostolic Nuncio to Haiti.

In July 2008 he was ordained Bishop of Suacia.

In July 2014 Archbishop Auza was appointed the Permanent Observer to the UN.

The following article was submitted by Archbishop Auza for this publication from his excerpt at the April 29, 2015 intervention of the Ninth Review Conference of the Treaty on the Non-Proliferation of Nuclear Weapons at the UN given on behalf of the Holy See.

Submission by the Most Reverend Bernardito C. Auza, Apostolic Nuncio, Permanent Observer of the Holy See to the United Nations, for Lois Nicolai's *Ordinary People, Extraordinary Times.*

"The Ethics of Peace and Solidarity instead of The Ethics of Mutually Assured Destruction"

2015 marks the seventieth anniversary of the nuclear bombing of Hiroshima and Nagasaki. The victims are still with us. The Hibakusha are a living testimony calling all of us to take the right decisions today if we do not want to face similar situations tomorrow. Hiroshima and Nagasaki should be a reminder on the importance ridding humanity of the risks of nuclear war. Nuclear disarmament is anchored in the dignity of the human person and in the collective recognition of the catastrophic humanitarian consequences of any nuclear detonation.

The world's nuclear arsenals still contain far too many of these weapons. The theory of nuclear deterrence is too ambiguous to be a stable and global basis of world security and international order. On the contrary, these weapons are per se inhumane and unethical. The hopes that have been placed by some in the system of deterrence as a strategy for preventing the use of nuclear weapons and for providing a stable security did not deliver the sort of peace and stability expected.

The risks of nuclear weapons are well known. The nuclear weapons states and non-nuclear states alike are aware of the exceptional instability caused by these weapons. The consequences of this instability are too important to be adopted as a basis for a genuine, peaceful and stable international order. Balance of terror is not the best basis for political, economic and cultural stability in the world.

The risks and the instability connected with the existence of nuclear weapons are an urgent call to take concrete and effective steps to address this situation by renewing collectively the commitment to nuclear nonproliferation and nuclear disarmament. There is no doubt that the safest and surest path toward non-use is the mutual and total renunciation of these weapons, and the effective dismantling of the infrastructure on which they depend. It is this vision and commitment of a future without nuclear weapons that ought to bring us together. The failure to translate in good faith the obligations contained in international non-proliferation treaties constitutes a real threat to the survival of humanity as a whole.

The discrimination between countries with and countries without nuclear weapons cannot remain permanent, as it was meant to be provisory. The status quo is unsustainable and undesirable. If it is unthinkable to imagine a world where nuclear weapons are available to all, it is reasonable to imagine, and to work collectively for, a world where nobody has them.

The very possession of nuclear weapons will continue to come at an enormous financial cost. The expenditures, current and projected, represent resources that could, and indeed should, be put toward the development of societies and people. Pope Francis put it strongly in his message to the President of the Vienna Conference on the humanitarian consequences of nuclear weapons in December 2014: "Spending on nuclear weapons squanders the wealth of nations. To prioritize such spending is a mistake and a misallocation of resources that would be far better invested in the areas of integral human development, education, health and the fight against extreme poverty. When these resources are squandered, the poor and the weak living on the margins of society pay the price."

To continue investing in the production and the modernization of nuclear weapons is not logical. Billions are wasted each year to develop and maintain stocks that will supposedly never be used.

The possession of nuclear weapons and the reliance on nuclear deterrence have a very negative impact on the inter-relations of states. Why is it that the security of some can only be met with a particular type of weapon whereas other States must ensure their security without them? Is it not urgent to revisit in a transparent and honest manner the definition made by States, especially the nuclear weapons states, of their national security?

We are all aware that the goal of a world without nuclear weapons is not easy to achieve. All human realities are difficult and complex. But this is neither a reason nor an excuse not to seek disarmament and implement the obligations undertaken in international treaties. For this, all energies and commitments are necessary. They are even more necessary in times of international tensions. The role of international organizations, religious communities, civil society, and academic institutions is vital not to let hope die, nor to let cynicism and realpolitik take over. Ethics based on the threat of mutually assured destruction is not worthy of future generations.

As Pope Francis wrote to the Vienna Conference on the humanitarian consequences of nuclear weapons: "Nuclear deterrence and the threat of mutually assured destruction cannot be the basis for an ethics of fraternity and peaceful coexistence among people and states. The youth of today and tomorrow deserve far more. They deserve a peaceful world order based on the unity of the human family, grounded on respect, cooperation, solidarity and compassion."

Archbishop Bernardito C. Auza is Permanent Observer of the Holy See to the United Nations. These remarks are excerpted from his April 29, 2015 intervention at the UN on behalf of the Holy See at the Ninth Review Conference of the Treaty on the Non-Proliferation of Nuclear Weapons.

HELEN CALDICOTT

www.helencaldicott.com

Helen Caldicott was a graduate of the University of Adelaide School of Medicine and was a faculty member of Harvard Medical School. In 1971 she played a major role in Australia's opposition to French atmospheric nuclear testing in the Pacific.

In 1974 she founded the Cystic Fibrosis Clinic at Adelaide Children's hospital.

While at Harvard in the 1980's, she helped to reinvigorate, as its president, the Physicians for Social Responsibility, an organization of 23,000 doctors committed to educating their colleagues about the dangers of nuclear power, nuclear weapons and nuclear war.

On trips abroad she helped start similar medical organizations in many countries.

In 1980 she founded the Women's Action for Nuclear Disarmament (WAND).

In 1985 the International Physicians for the Prevention of Nuclear War won the Nobel Peace Prize.

The author and/or editor of eight books including <u>Nuclear Madness</u>, <u>Missile Envy</u>, and most recently, <u>Sleepwalking to Armageddon</u>, she has been the recipient of many awards and honorary degrees, the subject of three award-winning documentary films, and was named one of the 20th Century's most influential women by the Smithsonian Institute.

THE MEDICAL AND ECOLOGICAL CONSEQUENCES OF FUKUSHIMA

Written By Helen Caldicott

Due to my personal concerns regarding the ignorance of the world's media and politicians about radiation biology after the dreadful accident at Fukushima in Japan, I organized a 2 day symposium at the NY Academy of Medicine on March 11 and 12, 2013, titled 'The Medical and Ecological Consequences of Fukushima,' which was addressed by some of the world's leading scientists, epidemiologists, physicists and physicians who presented their latest data and findings on Fukushima.

The Great Eastern earthquake, measuring 9.0 on the Richter scale, and the ensuing massive tsunami on the east coast of Japan induced the meltdown of three nuclear reactors within several days. During the quake, the external power supply was lost to the reactor complex and the pumps, which circulate up to one million gallons of water per minute to cool each reactor core, ceased to function. Emergency diesel generators situated below the plants kicked in, but these were soon swamped by the tsunami. Without cooling, the radioactive cores in units 1, 2 and 3 began to melt within hours. Over the next few days, all three cores (each weighing more than 100 tons) melted their way through six inches of steel at the bottom of their reactor vessels and oozed their way onto the concrete floor of the containment buildings. At the same time, the zirconium cladding covering thousands of uranium fuel rods reacted with water, creating hydrogen, which initiated hydrogen explosions in units 1, 2, 3 and 4.

Massive quantities of radiation escaped into the air and water – three times more noble gases (argon, xenon and krypton) than were released at Chernobyl, together with huge amounts of other volatile and non-volatile radioactive elements, including cesium, tritium, iodine, strontium, silver, plutonium, americium and rubidium. Eventually sea water was – and is still – utilized to cool the molten reactors.

Fukushima is now described as the greatest industrial accident in history.

The Japanese government was so concerned that they were considering plans to evacuate 35 million people from Tokyo, as other reactors including Fukushima Dainis on the east coast were also at risk. Thousands of people fleeing from the smoldering reactors were not notified where the radioactive plumes were travelling, despite the fact that there was a system in place to track the plumes. As a result, people fled directly into regions with the highest radiation concentrations, where they were exposed to high levels of whole-body external gamma radiation being emitted by the radioactive elements, inhaling radioactive air and swallowing radioactive elements. Unfortunately, inert potassium iodide was not supplied, which would have blocked the uptake of radioactive iodine by their thyroid glands, except in the town of Miharu. Prophylactic iodine was eventually distributed to the staff of Fukushima Medical University in the days after the accident, after extremely high levels of radioactive iodine – 1.9 million becquerels/kg were found in leafy vegetables near the University. Iodine contamination was widespread in leafy vegetables and milk, whilst other isotopic contamination from substances such as cesium is widespread in vegetables, fruit, meat, milk, rice, and tea in many areas of Japan.

The Fukushima meltdown disaster is not over and will never end. The radioactive fallout which remains toxic for hundreds to thousands of years covers large swathes of Japan and will never be "cleaned up." It will contaminate food, humans, and animals virtu-ally forever. I predict that the three reactors which experienced total meltdowns will never be dissembled or decommissioned. TEPCO (Tokyo Electric Power Company) – says it will take at least 30 to 40 years and the International Atomic Energy Agency predicts at least 40 years before they can make any progress because of the extremely high levels of radiation at these damaged reactors.

This accident is enormous in its medical implications. It will induce an epidemic of cancer as people inhale the radioactive ele-ments, eat radioactive food and drink radioactive beverages. In 1986, a single meltdown and explosion at Chernobyl covered 40% of the European land mass with radioactive elements. Already, according to a 2009 report published by the New York Academy of Sciences, over one million people have already perished as a direct result of this catastrophe. This is just the tip of the iceberg, because large parts of Europe and the food grown there will remain radioactive for hun-dreds of years.

Medical Implications of Radiation

Fact number one

No dose of radiation is safe. Each dose received by the body is cumulative and adds to the risk of developing malignancy or genetic disease.

Fact number two

Children are ten to twenty times more vulnerable to the car-cinogenic effects of radiation than adults. Females tend to be more sensitive compared to males, whilst fetuses and immuno-compro-mised patients are also extremely sensitive.

Fact number three

High doses of radiation received from a nuclear meltdown or from a nuclear weapon explosion can cause acute radiation sickness, with alopecia, severe nausea, diarrhea, and thrombocytopenia. Reports of such illnesses, particularly in children, appeared within the first few months after the Fukushima accident.

Fact number four

Ionizing radiation from radioactive elements and radiation emitted from X-ray machines and CT scanners can be carcinogenic. The latent period of carcinogenesis for leukemia is 5-10 years and solid cancers 15-80 years. It has been shown that all modes of cancer can be induced by radiation, as well as over 6000 genetic diseases now described in the medical literature.

But, as we increase the level of background radiation in our environment from medical procedures, X-ray scanning machines at airports, or radioactive materials continually escaping from nuclear reactors and nuclear waste dumps, we will inevitably increase the incidence of cancer as well as the incidence of genetic disease in future generations.

Conclusion

In summary, the radioactive contamination and fallout from nuclear power plant accidents will have medical ramifications that will never cease, because the food will continue to concentrate the radioactive elements for hundreds to thousands of years. This will induce epidemics of cancer, leukemia, and genetic disease. Already we are seeing such pathology and abnormalities in birds and insects, and because they reproduce very fast it is possible to observe disease caused by radiation over many generations within a relatively short space of time.

Pioneering research conducted by Dr Tim Mousseau, an evolutionary biologist, has demonstrated high rates of tumors, cataracts, genetic mutations, sterility, and reduced brain size amongst birds in the exclusion zones of both Chernobyl and Fukushima. What happens to animals will happen to human beings.

The Japanese government is desperately trying to "clean up" radioactive contamination. But in reality, all that can be done is collect it, place it in containers and transfer it to another location. It cannot be made neutral and it cannot be prevented from spreading in the future. Some contractors have allowed their workers to empty radioactive debris, soil and leaves into streams and other illegal places. The main question becomes: Where can they place the contaminated material to be stored safely away from the environment for thousands of years? There is no safe place in Japan for this to happen, let alone to store thousands of tons of high-level radioactive waste which rests precariously at the 54 Japanese nuclear reactors.

Last but not least, Australian uranium fueled the Fukushima reactors. Australia exports uranium for use in nuclear power plants to 12 countries, including the US, Japan, France, Britain, Finland, Sweden, South Korea, China, Belgium, Spain, Canada and Taiwan. 270,000 metric tons of deadly radioactive waste exists in the world today, with 12,000 metric tons being added yearly. (Each reactor manufactures 30 tons per year and there are over 400 reactors globally.)

This high-level waste must be isolated from the environment for one million years – but no container lasts longer than 100 years. The isotopes will inevitably leak, contaminating the food chain, inducing epidemics of cancer, leukemia, congenital deformities and genetic diseases for the rest of time.

This, then, is the legacy we leave to future generations so that we can turn on our lights and computers or make nuclear weapons. It was Einstein who said, "the splitting of the atom changed everything save mans' mode of thinking, thus we drift towards unparalleled catastrophe."

The question now is: Have we, the human species, the ability to mature psychologically in time to avert these catastrophes, or, is it in fact, too late?

Disclaimer: The views, opinions and perspectives presented in this article are those of the author alone and does not reflect the views of the Australian Medical Student Journal. The accuracy, completeness and validity of any statements made within this article are not guaranteed. We accept no liability for any errors or omissions.

PAUL K. CHAPPELL

www.peacefulrevolution.com | www.peaceliteracy.org

Paul K. Chappell is the Peace Leadership Director of the Nuclear Age Peace Foundation, an Iraq War veteran, a West Point graduate, an international speaker, and the author of five books.

He grew up in Alabama, the son of a half-black and half-white father who fought in the Korean and Vietnam wars and a Korean mother. Growing up in a violent household, Chappell has sought answers to the issues of war and peace, rage and trauma, and vision, purpose, and hope. His website is www.peacefulrevolution.com.

Paul Chappell graduated from West Point in 2002, was deployed to Iraq, and left active duty in November 2009 as a Captain. He is the author of the *Road to Peace* series, a seven-book series about waging peace, ending war, the art of living, and what it means to be human. The first five published books in this series are *Will War Ever End?*, *The End of War*, *Peaceful Revolution*, *The Art of Waging Peace*, and *The Cosmic Ocean*.

Chappell lectures across the country and internationally, and he also teaches courses and workshops on Peace Leadership.

PHAETON'S FOLLY: THE DANGEROUS REINS OF THE NUCLEAR CHARIOT

by Paul K. Chappell

✉ 🅵 🆈 🅎 Share

Pictured above: A mosaic from ancient Rome with the inscription "Know Thyself" in ancient Greek.

Technology and arrogance are a deadly combination. Thousands of years ago, people foresaw the dangers that arise when technology is corrupted by arrogance. In Greek mythology, Icarus and his father, Daedalus, were imprisoned in a tower, but they had a way to escape. Daedalus constructed two pairs of wings out of wax and feathers. Although he warned Icarus not to fly too close to the sun, Icarus did not listen. Blinded by his arrogance, he flew higher and higher until the wax holding his wings together melted. Icarus's wings were a technological marvel that gave him a chance at freedom, but his arrogant misuse of this technology caused him to fall into the ocean and die.

Greek mythology also tells us of Phaëton, whose father was the sun god Helios. Phaëton wanted to drive his father's sun chariot, but this arrogant desire led to a disaster. Helios was a mighty deity with the power to drive his sun chariot on a safe path across the sky, but Phaëton was half human and wanted to do what only a god could do. Unable to handle the reins, Phaëton lost control of the sun chariot and could not stop it from plunging toward the earth. Plato writes that "[Phaëton] burnt up all that was upon the earth, and was himself destroyed by a thunderbolt [from Zeus]."[i]

A painting by Peter Paul Rubens of Phaëton falling from the sky.

The heat from our sun is generated by a nuclear reaction deep within its core. Our sun's nuclear reaction is at a safe distance of 93 million miles away, but during the 1940s people began creating dangerous nuclear reactions on our planet. Just as Phaëton believed he could control the sun chariot, many believe we can control the thousands of nuclear weapons around the world. We have narrowly avoided nuclear annihilation in the past, and in the age of terrorism our grip on the nuclear reins is slipping.

If we lose control of the nuclear chariot we will suffer the same tragedy that befell Phaëton. And if any survive they too will write about how we "burnt up all that was upon the earth." The story of Icarus tells us that some technology, like flight, must be used responsibly or we will get ourselves killed. The tragedy of Phaëton tells us that some technology, like a nuclear weapons arsenal capable of destroying humanity, is a disaster waiting to happen in the hands of fallible human beings.[ii]

The ancient Greeks probably could not foresee weapons as destructive as nuclear weapons, but they were well aware of human imperfection. Our fallibility as human beings is what ultimately makes nuclear weapons so dangerous. According to John F. Kennedy, nuclear holocaust can result from accident, miscalculation, or madness, which are all products of human fallibility.

In ancient Greece, the words "Know thyself" were inscribed at the temple at Delphi. Today many people use this saying to emphasize the importance of introspection, but in ancient Greece this saying meant something different. Back then "Know thyself" meant that you should know what kind of creature you are.[iii] Know that you are not a god. Know the limitations that result from being human. Know that you are mortal and fallible. The ancient Greeks realized that human beings who don't know themselves in this way, who believe they are god-like, are extremely dangerous.

The only reason nuclear weapons are dangerous is because we are fallible. If we were infallible, perfect, and truly godlike, nuclear weapons would not be a problem. In fact, humanity would not have any problems.[iv]

Humanity's arrogance as a species is understandable. In religions throughout history, the sun has been depicted as either created by God, or the embodiment of God. Before Albert Einstein created his equation $E=mc^2$, nobody in the world knew how the sun shined. What kind of fuel source could allow an object to burn so brightly for so many eons? It was a great mystery. Many people reasoned that the sun must be using a fuel source much more powerful than wood, oil, or coal, but what could it be? Einstein's equation revealed that the sun's fuel came from a nuclear reaction that converted matter into energy. By learning this secret of the sun, humanity gained an ability that seemed god-like. In religions and mythologies around the world, only gods could control solar fire. By unlocking the mystery of solar fire, humanity gained control of the nuclear chariot, and with it we gained Phaëton's ability to annihilate ourselves and all those around us.

The story of nuclear weapons did not begin in 1945 with the dropping of two atomic bombs on Japan. The story of nuclear weapons began ages ago, because it reflects a deeper story about the human condition. It is a story about our timeless struggle to reconcile the reality of our fallibility with our desire to be god-like. Since no human is perfect, who can be trusted with weapons capable of annihilating most life on our planet? As John F. Kennedy realized, all political leaders are vulnerable to accident, miscalculation, or madness, which are all products of human fallibility. If political leaders were not vulnerable in this way, they would not be human.

Every religion, philosophy, and scientific school of thought recognizes that human beings are fallible and imperfect. Every technology and system we have ever created is also fallible and imperfect, just like us. There has never been a car, computer, or any human invention ever made that is perfect, invulnerable to error, and incapable of breaking. Nuclear weapons and the system that sustains them are imperfect, just like every technology and system that human beings have ever created.

Humanity's arrogant belief that it can control a vast nuclear weapons arsenal may lead to violence on an unprecedented scale, in the form of a nuclear holocaust. The word "hubris" was a Greek term that referred to wanton violence resulting from arrogance. In Greek mythology, the female deity Nemesis punished those guilty of hubris. If humanity loses control of the nuclear chariot, it will not just be nuclear weapons that cause our world to burn with solar fire. If the nuclear chariot wrecks our planet, it will also be because of fallibility, hubris, and the metaphorical goddess Nemesis. Nuclear weapons are a symptom of much deeper problems, such as the myth of nuclear deterrence and the confusion about what it means to be human.

[i] Plato, Timaeus, http://classics.mit.edu/Plato/timaeus.html.
[ii] This piece is adapted from my book *Peaceful Revolution*.

LINDA PENTZ GUNTER

www.beyondnuclear.org | www.BeyondNuclearInternational.org

Linda Pentz Gunter founded Beyond Nuclear in 2007 and serves as its international specialist as well as its media and development director. Prior to her work in anti-nuclear advocacy, she was a journalist for 20 years in print and broadcast, working for USA Network, Reuters, The Times (UK) and other US and international outlets.

Beyond Nuclear works to support grassroots, national and international efforts to phase out nuclear power in favor of safer renewable energy choices. It also draws attention to the perpetual link between nuclear power and the pathway to nuclear weapons and advocates for a global nuclear weapons ban. In creating Beyond Nuclear, Linda's goal was to reach beyond the immediate circle of committed anti-nuclear activists and engage those environmentalists concerned with climate change and the necessity to move away from fossil and fissile energy use.

In 2018, Linda launched a new web platform, BeyondNuclearInternational.org, which aims to reframe the anti-nuclear message through a more human lens. While focusing her writing on the Beyond Nuclear International site, Linda continues to write for Truthout, Counterpunch, The Ecologist and others. She makes occasional appearances as an expert on television and radio programs.

Originally from the UK, Linda has a BA Honors degree in English and Italian Literature from Warwick University where she also studied and wrote about film. In additional to her mother tongue she speaks Italian, French, German, Spanish and a touch of Welsh.

WE CAN RELY ON NEITHER LUCK NOR URANIUM FOREVER. CLOSING NUCLEAR POWER PLANTS IS THE ESSENTIAL WAY FORWARD

By Linda Pentz Gunter

On a sunny October day in 2009, a French border town was put under siege. There was no pandemic, but there was an invasion of sorts. Protesters against the continued operation of the Fessenheim nuclear power plant were streaming into town. French authorities weren't worried about their own citizens, but what they really feared were those "rioting" Germans.

We were in Colmar, a town in Alsace, a region that has historically been a source of conflict between France and Germany for more than a century, changing hands several times until finally becoming French again in the waning days of World War II.

Possibly unaware of this, but maybe guilty of watching too many news clips of German protesters at Gorleben, the French police locked Colmar down.

The original protest site in the central Place Rapp was moved to one on the outskirts of town, adjacent to the station. Helicopters circled overhead, police with dogs (yes, Alsatians) blocked intersections, and trucks with the word "horses" plastered on them idled in side streets.

On the morning of the protest, the only place to get a cup of coffee was in the local butcher shop. Everything else was closed. When the French close their cafes, you know something serious is going on.

Five thousand peace-loving people turned up, wearing sunshine yellow, singing songs, and carrying signs and generally shouting "hooray for our side" as per tradition.

And then, despite all the security, two protesters appeared on the roof of the bank building and unfurled a giant banner that read: "Nuclear kills the future." All the policemen and dogs and horses stood by, well, sheepishly, to mix animal metaphors.

Fessenheim finally began its phased shutdown process in 2020, closing one reactor in March, and the second one in June. But the French activists who had fought so long for this victory, did not crack open the champagne. They just let out a big sigh of relief, and then returned to the metaphorical barricades.

After all, Fessenheim's lethal inventory of radioactive waste remains on site atop an active seismic zone. An accident could still happen. And, most ominously, the French government has plans to turn Fessenheim into a "Technocentre" which proposes to "recycle" metal from the dismantled plant, and from others around Europe, into everyday household items like casseroles, toasters, stoves and boxsprings. It's the French government's twisted way of recategorizing nuclear as "renewable."

Nuclear reactors are closing everywhere. They are the fading dinosaurs of a 20th century technology that proved to be wildly expensive and failed to solve its nuclear waste problem. It was also responsible for some of the world's worst industrial accidents — most notably the nuclear meltdowns at Chernobyl in Ukraine and Fukushima, Japan.

In the U.S., the struggle to close the Indian Point nuclear power plant just 30 miles from New York City brought on similar challenges to those at Fessenheim. Indian Point shut down the first of its two remaining reactors on April 30, 2020, with a target closure date of April 30, 2021 for the other. The older Unit 1 closed in 1974.

Indian Point, like Fessenheim, also sits in a highly seismic area. Both Fessenheim and Indian Point have come close to disaster, an eventuality avoided only by luck. Just two months after our demonstration in Colmar, the Fessenheim plant suffered a serious loss of coolant accident. This came on the heels of countless incidents and safety shutdowns at the site.

At Indian Point, there was a close call after operators were allowed to put off the inspection of thousands of steam generator tubes — a key safety component — during a refueling outage. Several months later, in February 2000, a single steam generator tube ruptured at Indian Point Unit 2, releasing radioactivity into the environment. The situation could have been far more dangerous had the high-pressure rupture caused a cascading guillotine effect on neighboring tubes that would have led to a loss of coolant accident.

By necessity, nuclear power plants are located on bodies of water, from which they draw to cool the plant. At Indian Point, it is the Hudson River which the industry has abused for decades, not only with its heated water discharges but by drawing in and killing countless billions of fish. At Fessenheim it is a canal, sitting at higher grade than the nuclear plant, creating a serious risk of inundation should the protective wall between them fail.

The closures of Fessenheim, Indian Point, and at least a half dozen others in the US between 2014 and 2020, could not have come soon enough. Depending on luck to avert major disaster is an unsustainable path, just as the choice to continue the use of nuclear energy, reliant on a finite source of high-grade uranium for fuel, is also. Both luck, and the uranium, will eventually run out.

RICHARD FALK

www.richardfalk.worldpress.com | www.cpnn-world.org

Richard Falk is a professor emeritus of international law at Princeton University where he was a member of the faculty for 40 years.

He currently is Professor of Global Law, Queen Mary University, London.

He is co-author of ***Indefensible Weapons: The Political, and Psychological Case Against Nuclearism,*** and of ***On Nuclear Weapons: Denuclearization, Demilitarization and Disarmament***, published in 2019.

Professor Falk has been nominated annually for the Nobel Peace Prize since 2009. He is the Senior Vice President of the Nuclear Age Peace Foundation and served between 2008 – 2014 as the UN Special Rapporteur for Occupied Palestine.

CONTRIBUTION OF RICHARD FALK TO MEMOIR OF LOIS NICOLAI

It is a pleasure and honor to offer this small contribution to this exceptionally valuable portrayal of Lois Nicolai's genuinely extraordinary life journey on behalf of world peace. I am left unconvinced only by her claim of ordinariness, which strikes me as dramatically inconsistent with raising six children on her own, an undertaking that strikes me as extraordinary as do the impressive list of her many activities relating to peace and peacefulness. I will limit my comments to issues associated with arms control and disarmament as bearing on the approach taken by the U.S. Government, and its European allies, to the possession, deployment, doctrines, and development of nuclear weaponry.

It is often argued that arms control is a realistic approach that can be thought of as satisfying preconditions for negotiating a verified nuclear disarmament agreement, and having the added benefits of reducing risks of an accidental or mistaken use of nuclear weapons and of avoiding wasteful costs associated with arms races designed to maintain security in relation to adversaries.

There is some truth in this support for arms control, but such advocacy hides an important quite different part of the broader story. In addition to reducing risks and miscalculations, arms control seems to have as its primary goal bringing stability to world order *without* getting safely rid of this weaponry that poses threats to human wellbeing of catastrophe and even extinction. The more stable the overall political environment, the less incentive there would be to explore seriously a denuclearizing disarmament alternative. And this is not, as often alleged, because the risks of cheating and a renewal of nuclear competition is more dangerous than a world order in which the nuclear weapons states exercise prudence and prevent further proliferation of the weaponry.

Underlying this kind of justification for relegating the prospects of getting rid of nuclear weaponry to the most distant horizons – proclaiming it to be the 'ultimate' goal – is to signal that it is not really the goal at all except useful to keep disarmament advocates confused. The real story is that the national security establishment, at least in the U.S., and maybe elsewhere, *opposes* nuclear disarmament, for two interrelated reasons.

It gains prestige and leverage from 'nuclear apartheid' by which it perpetuates the vulnerability of all non-nuclear states, while asserting its geopolitical supremacy by 'enforcing' the Nonproliferation Treaty (NPT) against countries (e.g. Iran, North Korea) that seek such weaponry, and are perceived as hostile to Western interests while being complicit in evading proliferation controls for allies (Israel) and winking at nuclearization if the countries are too large to challenge (India, Pakistan).

Nuclear deployments and threats to use nuclear weapons confer geopolitical advantages and options on the nuclear weapons states, besides giving some security about the threats of being attacked. Qaddafi was undoubtedly correct when he said that Libya would not have been attacked in 2011 'had it possessed nuclear weapons', and Iraq in 2003 was likely attacked because it didn't have a nuclear deterrent.

This rationale for retaining nuclearism was starkly confirmed by the formal statement issued by the U.S., France, and the UK as to why they disagreed with the recent UN International Convention Against Nuclear Weapons (ICAN), emphasizing the positive role of nuclear weaponry in keeping the peace. In view of these considerations, why do NGO's in civil society continue to act as if they are working for nuclear disarmament when they embrace an arms control approach?

Above all, despite experience and evidence, 'the arms control first' community believes that reducing the size of the arsenal and agreeing not to develop some weapons systems are helpful measures on their own, as well also stepping stones to disarmament negotiations. Additionally, there is the belief that the retention of nuclear weapons is so entrenched that only arms control agreements are feasible and are better than nothing even if unrelated to a disarmament commitment. Finally, as arms control activism is concentrated in Washington, the only way to get a seat at the tables set by government is to shed the utopian image of disarmament advocacy and settle for what is feasible although it means dancing with the devil.

We can ask, then, where does this leave those dedicated to peace, and especially to avoiding any use of a nuclear weapon during a war? In my view, it is not appropriate to adopt an either/or position of saying no disarmament because unattainable or never arms control because it legitimates nuclear apartheid, and closes its eyes to geopolitical reliance on the leverage gained by wielding the weaponry. It is currently important to challenge public complacency about nuclear weaponry because these weapons have not been used since 1945, and to become attentive to the warnings of impending danger signaled by moving the highly credible Doomsday Clock of *The Bulletin of Atomic Scientists* to within 90 seconds to midnight, or closer to doomsday than it has ever been since established. In effect, it is delusional to suppose that we can indefinitely co-exist with this infernal weaponry.

It would also be helpful to call attention to the fact that although the NPT in Article Vl imposes an unconditional obligation of nuclear weapons states to engage in good faith nuclear disarmament negotiations as part of the agreement reached with other states to forego the nuclear weapons option.

This legal commitment was unanimously affirmed by the International Court of Justice in its Advisory Opinion delivered in 1996, and yet by continuing to invest heavily in the development of new nuclear weapons responsive to combat missions this central legal obligation is being violated.

Even if this legal commitment did not exist the idea of resting security on threats to retaliate by destroying many millions of innocent civilians and contaminating the atmosphere of the entire planet quite possibly causing what experts call 'a nuclear famine' and widespread disease. Such homicidal courses of action underline the immorality of resting security on such massive indiscriminating nuclear strikes that would fill the air with contaminating radioactivity. The UN ICAN Treaty, now formally ratified by 37 of the 50 States needed to bring the agreement into force is an important move in the right direction, and far more helpful than is an uncritical endorsement of this or that arms control proposal. There are arms control measures that can be supported in good conscience, including No First Use Declarations removing ambiguity from threats to use the weapons, and de-alerting measures that gives leaders more time to avoid accidental or unintended uses.

In the end, those who like Lois Nicolai are devoted to world peace need to take a stand against retaining nuclear weapons as an indispensable step toward achieving peace for all peoples on earth.

DR. REBECCA JOHNSON

www.acronym.org.uk

Dr. Rebecca Eleanor (RebEl) Johnson is a long-time feminist peace activist and Director of the Acronym Institute for Disarmament Diplomacy. Since 2009, as co-chair and co-founding first president of the International Campaign to Abolish Nuclear Weapons (ICAN), she prioritised her humanitarian disarmament work to achieve the 2017 Treaty on the Prohibition of Nuclear Weapons (TPNW), for which ICAN was awarded the 2017 Nobel Peace Prize.

While studying physics and chemistry, RebEl became a feminist in the 1970s, obtained her B.Sc from Bristol University, and then travelled solo through Europe, Africa and parts of Asia before teaching for two years in Japan. In 1981 she returned to study postgraduate politics at London University's School of Oriental and African Studies (SOAS) and became involved in anti-nuclear and peace campaigning. She lived at the Greenham Common Women's Peace Camp (1982-87) and served several sentences in Holloway and other prisons for nonviolent peace and justice actions. She also co-founded the Aldermaston Women's Peace Camp(aign) as an ongoing monthly camp outside Britain's primary nuclear bomb factory and participated in Women Working for a Nuclear Free and Independent Pacific, as well as CND (UK's Campaign for Nuclear Disarmament).

When the 1987 Intermediate Nuclear Forces (INF) Treaty ended the deployment of cruise missiles at Greenham, RebEl headed Greenpeace's international campaigns to ban nuclear testing and plutonium production. She participated in Women in Black protests in Jerusalem in 1989-90, followed by closer involvement with feminist anti-nationalist resisters in former Yugoslavia. In 1994, RebEl moved to Geneva to support peace-building objectives and work with NGOs and governments to achieve the 1996 Comprehensive Test Ban Treaty (CTBT).

The Acronym Institute was founded at this time, with its journal *Disarmament Diplomacy*, which has formed the core of her professional work ever since. She studied part time at London School of Economics (LSE) and received a Ph.D for her thesis on multilateral nuclear arms control negotiations. Dr Johnson's publications include: *Unfinished Business* on the CTBT; Trident and International Law: Scotland's Obligations (co-edited with Angie Zelter); Acronym reports and analyses on the Non-Proliferation Treaty (NPT) Review Process from 1994 onwards; and the humanitarian and security developments leading to the 2017 Treaty on the Prohibition of Nuclear Weapons. See www.acronym.org.uk and *OpenDemocracy*.

Dr Johnson currently serves on the International Panel on Fissile Materials (IPFM) and ICAN Steering Group. Previous roles include Senior Advisor for the International Weapons of Mass Destruction Commission (Blix Commission, 2004-2006), Vice Chair of the Board of the Bulletin of the Atomic Scientists (2001-7), co-coordinating the Faslane365 campaign, and serving as adviser to the United Nations, various governments, educational institutions and campaigns. Most recently she has become involved with Extinction Rebellion to persuade governments to treat climate destruction as a global emergency, and now serves on the Council.

BEYOND HIROSHIMA, GREENHAM, AND THE UN NUCLEAR BAN TREATY: A MEDITATION ON RADIATION

Rebecca Johnson's thoughts for Lois (May 2020)

In November 1982 I stood in Newbury Magistrates Court in England and gave testimony about the terrible blast, heat and nuclear radiation inflicted on the people of Hiroshima when the first atomic bomb – code-named "Little Boy" – exploded on August 6, 1945. I told the Court about my visit to Hiroshima two years before, while teaching in Japan, and described the terrible photos I saw in the peace museum, especially children suffering burns and radiation sickness. I told about meeting Hibakusha, and that I joined in their pledge – Never Again".

Together with a group of women from Wales, I was on trial for occupying the sentry box in the US Air Force base at Greenham Common a few months earlier. I had recently started living at the Greenham Women's Peace Camp, and this was my first ever nonviolent direct action for disarmament. Our purpose was to raise awareness of the need to ban and eliminate nuclear weapons, starting with the new generation of nuclear-armed cruise missiles that NATO and the Soviet Union were deploying in Europe. One of our group was a pregnant woman who gave evidence on how radiation affected children and babies in the womb. She spoke passionately about her need to protect her unborn child by stopping nuclear warmongers.

Nonetheless the magistrates found us guilty of "breach of the peace", using a 600-year-old law, and we were sent to London's Holloway Prison, following in the footsteps of the Suffragettes.

The next year I was on trial again after 44 women sneaked into the US base at dawn on New Year's morning and climbed to the top of the concrete silos under construction to house the cruise missiles. During our trial for "dancing on the silos", I met Rosalie Bertell, author of "No Immediate Danger", who came from Canada to give evidence on our behalf.

I had chosen to live outside the US nuclear base because I knew that if war was fought again with nuclear weapons humanity would face unspeakable horrors and even, perhaps, extinction, through nuclear winter and mass famine. From Rosalie and Dr Alice Stewart who also gave expert evidence, I learnt much more. They spoke of how – even before another nuclear weapon is used – ionizing radiation from all links in the nuclear chain are putting humanity, our planet, and our future generations at risk.

My life was changed by what these two brilliant women told us. I always knew that nuclear weapons were immoral and must be banned and eliminated. That is why I went to Greenham. But as a young physics student concerned about acid rain and pollution in the 1970s, I had believed that nuclear energy could be beneficial for the world if we were only smart enough to "solve the nuclear waste problem". But I gave up physics when I understood that military purposes underpinned "atoms for peace", and that nuclear energy could never be the answer to the laudable quest for "cheap, safe and clean" energy. In Court in February 1983, Rosalie Bertell and Dr Alice Stewart convinced me not only to campaign for nuclear disarmament, but also to raise awareness to stop the cumulative damage from "low level" radiation as well as nuclear explosions.

From uranium mining to nuclear power and nuclear testing, ionizing radiation from fissile materials such as uranium and plutonium are insidiously contaminating our environment, killing people all over the world, and creating threats for future generations.
For five years I lived outside the nuclear base at Greenham, until the 1987 Intermediate Nuclear Forces (INF) Treaty removed the cruise and SS20 missiles. Having by then dedicated my life to making the world as nuclear free as possible, I got a job for some years with Greenpeace, to lead their international test ban campaign. I

organized protests at various nuclear test sites and spoke to indigenous people, downwinders and military veterans whose lives had been blighted by nuclear testing.

These included: Aboriginal people contaminated by British testing; Polynesians who suffered from American, British and French testing in the Pacific; Kazakhs in villages near the Soviet Union's huge Semipalatinsk test site, and indigenous Nenets herders forced to leave Novaya Zemlya to escape further Soviet testing in the Arctic; downwinders from the Nevada Test Site, including Western Shoshone and rural communities from Utah to North Dakota (where I'd lived as a Hutterite child in the 1950s). I also spoke to nomadic Tauregs affected by French testing in Alderia and indigenous Uighurs from Xinjiang, where China's Lop Nor testing took place until 1996.

Together with disarmament campaigners, nuclear survivors, and the Conference on Disarmament, we managed to get the Comprehensive Test Ban Treaty (CTBT) adopted in 1996, with 184 Member States. Though a fatal Achilles Heel inserted in its entry-into-force provisions has prevented it from taking full legal effect, the CTBT felt like a big milestone towards making the world nuclear free.

After going back to grassroots activism in 2006-07 at the Faslane nuclear base in Scotland, (where UK nuclear armed Trident weapons are deployed), I took the lead in establishing the Geneva office of the International Campaign to Abolish Nuclear Weapons (ICAN). Together with international physcians, Women's International League for Peace and Freedom and a handful of progressive governments, we built the movement that brought the 2017 Treaty on the Prohibition of Nuclear Weapons (TPNW, aka 'Nuclear Ban Treaty) to fruition.

Fundamentally, the TPNW bans the use, production and deployment of nuclear weapons and requires their total abolition, with provisions to implement the Treaty and verifiably eliminate the weapons safely and securely. But of equal importance is how the Treaty's preamble frames these prohibitions and obligations in feminist-humanitarian terms:

"*Cognizant* that the catastrophic consequences of nuclear weapons cannot be adequately addressed, transcend national borders, pose grave implications for human survival, the environment, socioeconomic development, the global economy, food security and the health of current and future generations, and have a disproportionate impact on women and girls, including as a result of ionizing radiation…"

When it was adopted by the UN General Assembly, I felt as if my life as a feminist peace campaigner was coming full circle. Yet, as I write this piece for Lois in May 2020, Donald Trump is wantonly wrecking our treaties, from the INF Treaty to the Paris Climate Accord and CTBT, while I am locked down in my 6th floor flat. All around us, neighbours, friends and family members struggle with Covid-19, and some die.

Pandemics like this have been warned about for years, just as nuclear dangers, pollution and climate destruction are warned about. But most people don't want to believe these will result in real catastrophes or affect us personally. As the coronavirus numbers mount up, I remember my friend Setsuko Thurlow, whose schoolfriends were incinerated when the atomic bomb was dropped on Hiroshima, reminding us all: "each and every one of them had a name, and people who loved them deeply".

The political-military-industrial and bureaucratic-academic establishments are struggling to keep up with what is happening. Like radiation, Covid-19 is an invisible killer that spreads into our lungs and blood, changing our lives and futures forever. As in the Cold War, when I grew up under the ever-present Damoclean threat of nuclear annihilation, people desperately want to feel secure. But this isn't a war with an enemy you can defeat with nuclear bombs, guns, or violence.

We need to rethink security and put health, education, climate justice and sustainable food and energy first. The true defences we need are the skills and dedication of doctors, nurses, teachers, scientists, and all those poorly paid women who feed and care for millions of vulnerable people. And we need poetry, music, writers and peace activists to transform this world and hold governments to account.

JONATHAN GRANOFF

www.gsinstitute.org

Jonathan Granoff is an International Advocate emphasizing the legal, ethical, and spiritual dimensions of human development, peace and security, and ending threats posed by nuclear weapons.

He serves as president of the Global Security Institute. The institute is dedicated to strengthening international security based on cooperation and respect for the rule of law. Its focus is on nuclear arms control, nonproliferation, and disarmament. The team includes former heads of state, distinguished diplomats and politicians, committed celebrities, religious leaders, Nobel Peace laureates, disarmament and legal experts, and concerned citizens. All members are united by a common purpose – to create a world free of nuclear weapons.

Mr. Granoff is Chair of the Task Force on Nuclear Non-Proliferation of the International Law Section of the American Bar Association.

He also serves on numerous governing and advisory boards, including the Lawyers' Committee on Nuclear Policy, the Fortune Forum, the Jane Goodall Institute, and the Middle Powers Initiative.

Over the years, he has given expert testimony in Congress and at the UN and was nominated for the Nobel Peace Prize in 2014. See www.gsinstitute.org

THOUGHTS ON INNER ASPECTS REGARDING THE ELIMINATION OF NUCLEAR WEAPONS:

Thoughts on Inner Aspects Regarding the Elimination of Nuclear Weapons

Work to achieve nuclear disarmament may appear as only an external, public pursuit. It has taught me much about the value of a prayerful inner life and the centrality of love and prayer. Since I speak as a full-time political activist rather than as a religious leader, readers need not fear that my goal is proselytization for one religion or another when I say that the transformative power of prayer is crucial to our personal growth and political struggle for global peace.

The evidence of real prayer is whether it opens the heart to love, regardless of whether we pray quietly, out loud, within a tradition, out of a tradition, facing the east, the west, up or down. If it's prayer, it opens the heart to God's love. If it doesn't, it's not prayer.

As Bawa Muhaiyadeen said:

"If each of you will open your heart, your action, your wisdom, and your conduct, and look within, you will see that every face is your face ... all sorrow is your sorrow.... When that state develops inside you, that is God's love ... If that love develops, you will not hurt any other living thing. You will not cause pain, you will not reject any life...Because if you hurt anyone, it will hurt you."

Feeling the joy and sorrow of others brings one into an active sense of responsibility, awakens conscience, and leads to action. Being effective in the realm of action means using skills, intelligence, political insight, and practical knowledge, but always in the service of that greater responsibility to the Source.

Without developing an inner character based on love and compassion, the instability of the mind, the harshness of the world, and the challenge of facing our mortality will breed fear. Fear is responsible for closing down dialogue and denying our interconnectedness. Fear too often can trump reason. But fear cannot overcome authentic experience-based love.

A culture that overemphasizes competition reinforces a false sense of disconnectedness. Reliance on science and technology to solve human dilemmas does not lead to peace. The threats of nuclear annihilation and war certainly give anyone adequate reasons for fear. The modern world does little to remind us of our humanity.

General Omar Bradley, a man familiar with the horrors of battle said it clearly: "We live in an age of nuclear giants and ethical infants, in a world that has achieved brilliance without wisdom, power without conscience. We've solved the mystery of the atom and forgotten the lessons of the Sermon on the Mount."

When fear is central to the public discourse we can be sure the least insightful among us will use it to profit from cycles of armaments and war, which reinforce the causes of fear. In fact, since the end of the Cold War, the world has spent more than $10 trillion on armaments. The United States has recently committed to spending another $1 Trillion to modernize its nuclear arsenal and every state with these devices, nine in all (China, U.S., France, U.K., Russia, Israel, Pakistan, India, and North Korea) are either modernizing or expanding their arsenals, or doing both.

A mere 100 nuclear explosions would propel a sufficient amount of debris into the atmosphere to so degrade the climate that billions would starve from famine and render civilization a memory. The most sophisticated scientific enterprise ever developed arises from fear and expresses the apex of destruction.

Some of us have experienced the opening of the heart and felt the unity of humanity. We know that love is the manifest dynamic that weaves together the mysterious infinite web of life of which we are but a part. We know that there is no power greater than the power of love.

From the glorious place of inner courage and freedom, we know the cycle can be changed: no more fear inside and no more squandering of public assets based on illusory quests for power. We know that the gift of this faithful insight is spreading, despite the pockets where violence has disrupted society and despite the pornography of trivia and stupidity of the mass media.

People everywhere are feeling the coming of something new, something better and more human. There is a force that causes the seed to become a flower. It cannot be denied its expression.

When individuals act from the place of the open heart, everyday life is enriched with the sacred; when groups act with resonance from this treasure, social change for peace and justice emerges. This is not a new insight. It is just a reminder that love is the healing force for each person and the strongest force for social change, even today.

Jonathan Granoff

CYNTHIA LAZAROFF

www.globalzero.org | www.cynthialazaroff.com

CYNTHIA LAZAROFF

Cynthia Lazaroff is the founder of NuclearWakeUpCall.Earth and Women Changing Nuclear Policy. She is an award-winning documentary filmmaker and author of *Dawn of a New Armageddon*, a personal account of her experience during the Hawaii missile scare amidst escalating nuclear dangers, published in the *Bulletin of the Atomic Scientists* on Hiroshima Day.

Cynthia is engaged in Track II citizen diplomacy and mediation efforts with Russia and has founded groundbreaking U.S.-Russian exchange initiatives since the early 1980s. She has produced films including *U.S.-Russia Relations: Quest for Stability*, a seven-part documentary series, and *Mourning Armageddon*, a music video featuring Hawaii artist Makana, both released in 2019.

Previously, Cynthia served as Director of Creative Affairs at Armand Hammer Productions where she developed mini-series such as *Mother Russia* for HBO *The Cuban Missile Crisis* for NBC and the award-winning *Hiroshima* for Showtime. Cynthia co-produced *The Challenge of the Caucasus,* featuring the first joint ascent of Mount Elbrus, Europe's highest peak, by Soviet and American youth whom she co-led to the summit. In 1983, at the height of Cold War tensions, Cynthia co-founded the US-USSR Youth Exchange Program where she pioneered exchanges in art, literature, theater, education, film. sports, wilderness adventures, urban leadership and environmental service.

This article was originally published by Global Zero, globalzero.org
on February 6, 2019 and is reprinted here with their permission.

One Year After We Thought the Doomsday Clock Struck Midnight
by Cynthia Lazaroff

Last January, I was one of over a million people in Hawaii whose cell phone lit up with
this message:

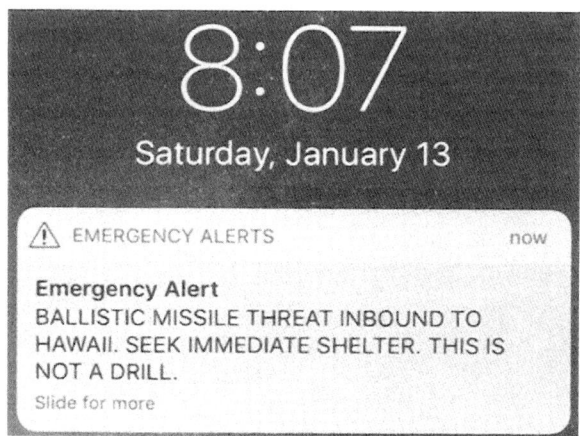

I spent 38 minutes in cell-splitting terror, thinking I was about to be hit by a nuclear
missile. After I got a confirmation from local authorities that we should take shelter, it
became gut-punch real. I did not know whether this was one or two missiles from North
Korea launched at the height of the "fire and fury" or the start of a full-scale nuclear war
with Russia due to accident, miscalculation, blunder. I felt the existential terror of The
Doomsday Clock striking midnight, the beginning of the end of the world as we know it,
of everyone and everything we know and love. It was an awakening to what is at stake
that lives inside my body, in my cellular memory to this day.

I have chronicled our family's moment-to-moment experience of those 38 minutes in
Dawn of a new Armageddon in the Bulletin of the Atomic Scientists. To make the nuclear
threat real, I take groups through simulations of getting an emergency alert on their cell
phones warning of a nuclear attack just like we got in Hawaii. Wherever they are –
Moscow, New York, Washington, Seoul, Islamabad.

And I share what top nuclear experts have taught me. That this is our planet's most
dangerous time. That nuclear dangers are escalating and the risk of a nuclear exchange
due to bluster, accident or miscalculation is greater than at any time in history – even
greater than during the peak crisis moments of the Cold War. That as my dear friend
Hawaii artist Makana says in his haunting new music video, "We are in bed with
annihilation."

Former nuclear war planner turned activist Daniel Ellsberg says in his book *The Doomsday Machine: Confessions of a Nuclear War Planner* that the human race is "not a species that can be trusted with nuclear weapons." History is proving this out. As I write this, the U.S. and Russia have just announced their withdrawal from the INF Treaty, a centerpiece for arms control and strategic stability that eliminated an entire class of nuclear weapons, reduced the risk of a nuclear exchange in Europe, brought an end to the old Cold War and opened the pathway for other groundbreaking arms control agreements like START I, resulting in the largest reductions in U.S. and Soviet/Russian nuclear arsenals in history.

With the collapse of INF and the expiration of New START looming on the horizon, we are entering an unimaginably deadly new arms race with Russia and fueling a new one with China. This is leading to a nuclear Wild West free-for-all of unprecedented danger, further escalating the risk of blundering into an unintended nuclear war. For so many of us who lived through the Cold War together, including dozens of dear Russian friends in Moscow and St. Petersburg, this is heartbreaking, a déjà vu nightmare – in the words of my 82 year-old Russian screenwriter friend Tanya, "sheer idiocy."

INF has collapsed not only due to U.S. ire over Russia's prohibited 9M729 cruise missile and Russian claims that the U.S. is violating the treaty because its Aegis Missile Defense System on Russia's borders is capable of launching Tomahawk cruise missiles. INF has also collapsed because the United States has not had a real nuclear dialogue with Russia for years now, not since the U.S. cut off most talks with Moscow after the events in Ukraine in 2014. Without ongoing talks with Russia, the U.S. will not be able to fix INF, extend New START, or make progress on reducing a host of other nuclear dangers.

Even at the most dangerous moments of the Cold War – despite deep ideological differences – the United States had a constant dialogue with Russia, an insulated, safe space for talks on arms control. Today the U.S. shuns a dialogue with Russia on nuclear security at our own, and humanity's, peril. In the words of former U.S. Secretary of Defense William Perry, "Because we don't understand the dangers we make no serious attempt to repair the hostility between the United States and Russia and so we are allowing ourselves to sleepwalk into a nuclear catastrophe. We must wake up."

Former California Governor Jerry Brown says that U.S. politicians must hold open "a channel of nuclear dialogue" with Russia. The United States must not hold these conversations hostage to political differences, but instead must talk and work with Russia and all nuclear powers to reduce the nuclear risk and move towards the eventual elimination of nuclear weapons.

One year after we thought the Doomsday Clock struck midnight in Hawaii, I am heartened by the growing grassroots movement emerging across the U.S. focused on transforming nuclear policy. There are people and politicians waking up to the nuclear danger and aligning around steps to be taken and legislation to be adopted in a way that we have not seen since the Nuclear Freeze movement of the 1980s. Congressman Adam Smith, new chair of the House Armed Services Committee, has taken a strong stand against the Trump Administration's Nuclear Posture Review, which supports a new low-yield nuclear warhead and leaves the door open for nuclear use against non-nuclear attacks. Smith and many of his colleagues in the House and Senate have introduced bold legislation for No First Use of nuclear weapons, restricting presidential

launch authority, defunding low-yield nuclear weapons development and prohibiting funding for short and intermediate-range nuclear missiles that violate INF until the Trump Administration meets certain conditions. See The Nuclear Playbook to learn more.

I came of age in the 1980s when I was part of a mass global movement of men and women, youth and children that transcended religious, racial, ethnic, gender, cultural, socio-economic and partisan divides. We were all united around one overarching common goal – preventing a nuclear war and creating a secure future for ourselves, our children. Dr. Bernard Lown, who accepted the Nobel Peace Prize in 1985 on behalf of the International Physicians to Prevent Nuclear War, said, "Politicians need to be compelled by people whose lives are in jeopardy." We the people united and compelled our leaders to transform nuclear policy in the 1980s. We can and must do so again today.

This article was originally published by Global Zero, globalzero.org on February 6, 2019 and is reprinted here with their permission.

FRANK VON HIPPEL

www.princeton.edu | www.thebulletin.org

Frank von Hippel, a nuclear physicist, is a Senior Research Physicist and Professor of Public and International Affairs emeritus at Princeton University where, in 1975, he cofounded and cochaired, for three decades, what is now Princeton's Program on Science and Global Security.

During 1983–1990, Professor von Hippel worked with President Gorbachev's science advisor, Evgenyi Velikhov, to develop a number of successful initiatives to end nuclear testing and the production of plutonium and highly enriched uranium for weapons, part of the Freeze agenda.

In 2006, Professor von Hippel cofounded the nongovernmental International Panel on Fissile Materials (IPFM) and cochaired it for its first nine years. The IPFM includes experts from eighteen countries and develops proposals for initiatives to reduce global stocks of plutonium and HEU and the numbers of locations where they can be found.

Professor von Hippel has advised U.S. Administrations and Congress on nuclear security issues since the Carter Administration.

During 1993–1994, he served as Assistant Director for National Security in the White House Office of Science and Technology Policy and played a major role in developing a number of US–Russian cooperative nuclear initiatives.

Frank was an active member of our Princeton-based World Citizen Diplomats citizen diplomacy organization throughout the 1990s.

CITIZEN ACTIVISM AGAINST THE NUCLEAR THREAT

Citizen Activism Against the Nuclear Threat

Frank von Hippel

[Contribution to Lois Nicolai's *Ordinary People, Extraordinary Times*, 13 Sept. 2015]

Lois Nicolai's wonderful account comes from an amazing period in American history when many ordinary citizens decided that the danger was so great that they had to get involved in stopping the nuclear arms race – which they did.

The uprising was fueled by irresponsible statements about nuclear war by officials of the new Reagan Administration, which took office in 1981. These new appointees had been members of the Committee on the Present Danger that had been warning that the U.S. was falling behind in the nuclear arms race and was in mortal danger of a Soviet first nuclear strike. The Committee argued that the Soviet leadership believed that it could fight and win a nuclear war. When President Reagan won the 1980 election, he appointed 33 members of the Committee to high-level positions in his administration, including as National Security Advisor, Secretary of State, Director of the CIA, and numerous senior positions in the Department of Defense.

It turned out that some of these appointees shared the belief that they had been imputing to the Soviet Union, that it would be possible to survive a nuclear war. T.K. Jones, the Reagan Administration's Deputy Under Secretary of Defense for strategic and theater nuclear forces famously said, "If there are enough shovels to go around, everybody's going to make it".

Such reckless statements galvanized an uprising that mobilized in the United States behind a call to freeze the nuclear arms race. In 1982, one million people came out to a single demonstration in support of a Freeze and that November citizens in nine states, the District of Columbia, and 37 cities and counties voted for a Freeze in referenda. In Europe a similar mass movement rose up against the deployment of a new generation of Soviet and U.S. nuclear missiles in Eastern and Western Europe.

President Reagan responded by shifting from his advocacy of a nuclear buildup to a call for the nation's scientists to join in a Strategic Defense Initiative (quickly dubbed by critics as "Star Wars") that would make nuclear missiles "impotent and obsolete."

In Moscow, Mikhail Gorbachev was impressed by the citizen uprisings in the U.S. and Western Europe and, in August 1985, soon after he was appointed General Secretary of the Soviet Communist Party, initiated a unilateral Soviet moratorium on nuclear testing. The Reagan Administration refused to join in and two years later, the Soviet Union resumed testing. The Democrat-led U.S. Congress was impressed, however and started to press for a nuclear test ban.

In 1989, in Khazakhstan, where most of the Soviet tests were being conducted, an underground test vented and the famous Khazakh poet, Olzas Suleimenov, went on television to call into being the "Nevada-Semipalatinsk" movement to end nuclear testing in both countries. Nuclear testing ended in the Soviet Union in 1990 the U.S in 1992.

Long before then, in 1985, 1987 and 1988, Gorbachev and Reagan put out joint summit statements that included the following sentence, "A nuclear war cannot be won and must never be fought."

Such is the power of an aroused citizenry.

Unfortunately, the citizens' movements largely demobilized with the end of the Cold War in 1989 and gradually the momentum of the nuclear arms reductions that had been launched in response to their pressure dissipated. Today, the global nuclear arsenal is much smaller than it was – about 10,000 warheads versus about 65,000 in the mid-1980s -- but still large enough to destroy civilization tens of times over. And, instead of focusing on further reductions, the five nuclear weapon states, which also happen to be the permanent members of the United Nations Security Council (the U.S., Russia, China, France and the UK) are all modernizing their nuclear "deterrents" while India, Pakistan and North Korea are all building up the sizes of their stockpiles. (I don't know whether the ninth nuclear weapon state, Israel, is still building up.)

So I pray that another anti-nuclear citizen's movement will rise again to carry us forward toward nuclear disarmament.

In the meantime, I thank Lois and all the other citizen activists who got us this far.

ALICE SLATER

www.worldbeyondwar.org | www.wagingpeace.org

Alice serves on the Board of World Beyond War and is a UN NGO Representative of the Nuclear Age Peace Foundation.

She is on the Board of the Global Network Against Weapons and Nuclear Power in Space, the Global Council of Abolition 2000, and the Advisory Board of Nuclear Ban-US, supporting the mission of the International Campaign to Abolish Nuclear Weapons which won the 2017 Nobel Peace Prize for its work in realizing the successful UN negotiations for a Treaty for the Prohibition of Nuclear Weapons.

She began her long quest for peace on earth as a suburban housewife, when she organized Eugene McCarthy's presidential challenge to Johnson's illegal war in Vietnam in her local community. As a member of the Lawyers Alliance for Nuclear Arms Control, she travelled to Russia and China on numerous delegations engaged in ending the arms race and banning the bomb.

She is a member of the NYC Bar Association and served on the People's Climate Committee-NYC, working for 100% Green Energy by 2030.

She has written numerous articles and op-eds, with frequent appearances on local and national media.

Hiroshima Unlearned:

Time to Tell the Truth About US Relations with Russia and Ban the Bomb

By Alice Slater

August 6th and 9th mark 74 years since the atomic bombing of Hiroshima and Nagasaki, where only one nuclear bomb dropped on each city caused the deaths of up to 146,000 people in Hiroshima and 80,000 people in Nagasaki. Today, with the US decision to walk away from the 1987 Intermediate-Range Nuclear Force (INF) negotiated with the Soviet Union, we are once again staring into the abyss of one of the most perilous nuclear challenges since the height of the Cold War.

With its careful verification and inspections, the INF Treaty eliminated a whole class of missiles that threatened peace and stability in Europe. Now the US is leaving the treaty on the grounds that Moscow is developing and deploying a missile with a range prohibited by the treaty. Russia denies the charges and accuses the US of violating the treaty. The US rejected repeated Russian requests to work out the differences in order to preserve the Treaty.

The US withdrawal should be seen in the context of the historical provocations visited upon the Soviet Union and now Russia by the United States and the nations under the US nuclear "umbrella" in NATO and the Pacific. The US has been driving the nuclear arms race with Russia from the dawn of the nuclear age:

In 1946 Truman rejected Stalin›s offer to turn the bomb over to the newly formed UN under international supervision, after which the Russians made their own bomb.

Reagan rejected Gorbachev's offer to give up Star Wars as a condition for both countries to eliminate all their nuclear weapons when the wall came down and Gorbachev released all of Eastern Europe from Soviet occupation, miraculously, without a shot.

The US pushed NATO right up to Russia's borders, despite promises when the wall fell that NATO would not expand it one inch eastward of a unified Germany.

Clinton bombed Kosovo, bypassing Russia's veto in the UN Security Council and violating the UN treaty we signed never to commit a war of aggression against another nation unless under imminent threat of attack.

Clinton refused Putin's offer to each cut our massive nuclear arsenals to 1000 bombs each and call all the others to the table to negotiate for their elimination, provided we stopped developing missile sites in Romania.

Bush walked out of the 1972 Anti-Ballistic Missile Treaty and put the new missile base in Romania with another to open shortly under Trump in Poland, right in Russia's backyard.

Bush and Obama blocked any discussion in 2008 and 2014 on Russian and Chinese proposals for a space weapons ban in the consensus-bound Committee for Disarmament in Geneva.

Obama's rejected Putin›s offer to negotiate a treaty to ban cyber war.

Trump now walked out of the INF Treaty.

From Clinton through Trump, the US never ratified the 1992 Comprehensive Test Ban Treaty as Russia has, and has performed more than 20 underground sub-critical tests on the Western Shoshone's sanctified land at the Nevada test site. Since plutonium is blown up with chemicals that don't cause a chain reaction, the US claims these tests don't violate the treaty.

Obama, and now Trump, pledged over one trillion dollars for the next 30 years for two new nuclear bomb factories in Oak Ridge and Kansas City, as well as new submarines, missiles, airplanes, and warheads!

What has Russia had to say about these US affronts to international security and negotiated treaties?

Putin at his State of the Nation address in March 2018 said:

I will speak about the newest systems of Russian strategic weapons that we are creating in response to the unilateral withdrawal of the United States of America from the Anti-Ballistic Missile Treaty and the practical deployment of their missile defense systems both in the US and beyond their national borders.

I would like to make a short journey into the recent past. Back in 2000, the US announced its withdrawal from the Anti-Ballistic Missile Treaty. Russia was categorically against this. We saw the Soviet-US ABM Treaty signed in 1972 as the cornerstone of the international security system. Under this treaty, the parties had the right to deploy ballistic missile defense systems only in one of its regions. Russia deployed these systems around Moscow, and the US around its Grand Forks land-based ICBM base. Together with the Strategic Arms Reduction Treaty, the ABM treaty not only created an atmosphere of trust but also prevented either party from recklessly using nuclear weapons, which would have endangered humankind, because the limited number of ballistic missile defense systems made the potential aggressor vulnerable to a response strike.

We did our best to dissuade the Americans from withdrawing from the treaty.

All in vain. The US pulled out of the treaty in 2002. Even after that we tried to develop constructive dialogue with the Americans. We proposed working together in this area to ease concerns and maintain the atmosphere of trust. At one point, I thought that a compromise was possible, but this was not to be. All our proposals, absolutely all of them, were rejected. And then we said that we would have to improve our modern strike systems to protect our security.

Despite promises made in the 1970 Non-Proliferation Treaty (NPT) that the five nuclear weapons states--US, UK, Russia, France, China--would eliminate their nuclear weapons while all the other nations of the world promised not to get them (except for India, Pakistan, and Israel, which also acquired nuclear weapons), there are still nearly 14,000 nuclear bombs on the planet. All but 1,000 of them are in the US and Russia, while the seven other countries, including North Korea, have about 1000 bombs between them. If the US and Russia can't settle their differences and honor their promise in the NPT to eliminate their nuclear weapons, the whole world will continue to live under what President Kennedy described as a nuclear Sword of Damocles, threatened with unimaginable catastrophic humanitarian suffering and destruction.

To prevent a nuclear catastrophe, in 2017, 122 nations adopted a new Treaty for the Prohibition of Nuclear Weapons (TPNW). It calls for a ban on nuclear weapons just as the world had banned chemical and biological weapons. The ban treaty provides a pathway for nuclear weapons states to join and dismantle their arsenals under strict and effective verification. The International Campaign to Abolish Nuclear Weapons, which received the Nobel Peace Prize for its efforts, is working for the treaty to enter into force by enrolling 50 nations to ratify the treaty. As of today, 70 nations have signed the treaty and 24 have ratified it, although none of them are nuclear weapons states or the US alliance states under the nuclear umbrella.

With this new opportunity to finally ban the bomb and end the nuclear terror, let us tell the truth about what happened between the US and Russia that brought us to this perilous moment and put the responsibility where it belongs to open up a path for true peace and reconciliation so that never again will anyone on our planet ever be threatened with the terrible consequences of nuclear war.

Here are some actions you can take to ban the bomb:

- Support the ICAN Cities Appeal to take a stand in favor of the ban treaty
- Ask your member of Congress to sign the ICAN Parliamentary Pledge
- Ask the US Presidential Candidates to pledge support for the Ban Treaty and cut Pentagon spending
- Support the Don't Bank on the Bomb Campaign for nuclear divestment
- Support the Code Pink Divest From the War Machine Campaign
- Distribute Warheads To Windmills, How to Pay for the Green New Deal, a new studey addressing the need to prevent the two greatest dangers facing our planet: nuclear annihilation and climate destruction.

KARIPBEK KUYUKOV

www.kuyukov.com

My name is Karipbek Kuyukov and I was born on July 18, 1968, in a village called Yegindybulak, Kazakhstan. My village is about a hundred kilometers from the former Semipalatinsk nuclear test site. Before me, there was a girl and a boy who didn't live to be even one year old in our family. My parents have lived and worked in this village all their lives and were firsthand witnesses to the nuclear tests. I eventually went to school in Leningrad, which is now Saint Petersburg, because there was a prosthetics institute located there. I also studied in the Volgograd and Orlovsky Oblsasts in Russia. After graduating high school, I enrolled into a bookkeeping course at a college in Zagorsk, in the Moscow Oblast, and graduated in 1987.

Enclosed is my contribution to Lois Nicolai's book.

Note from the author: On February 5, 1992, I received a telephone call from the Kremlin Operator in Moscow, connecting me with Olzhas Suleimenov's translator, Vladimir Iakimets. I had met both Olzhas and Vladimir the year before in Washington D.C. when they were participating in the Tripartite Delegation of Parliament Members working on a moratorium to stop nuclear testing throughout the world.

Vladimir explained that Olzhas wanted to send seven Kazakh radiation survivors to attend a three-day conference in the desert of Las Vegas, NV, to join with the American citizens' voices to stop nuclear testing. He said he would fly them from Moscow to NYC and would take the seven of them from Princeton, NJ to Las Vegas, NV for this meeting. One of the seven was Karipbek, a young survivor born with no arms. On March 31, I greeted them at Kennedy Airport and met Karipbek for the first time. I spent an entire month with him, and to this day he is a constant inspiration for me. Following is his story in his own words.

AUTOBIOGRAPHY

My name is Karipbek Kuyukov, I was born on July 18,1968 in the village called Yegindybulak, Kazakhstan, about 100 kilometers from the former Semipalatinsk nuclear test site. Before me there was a girl and a boy who didn't live to one year in our family. My parents have lived and worked in the village and were firsthand witnesses of nuclear tests. I went to school in Leningrad (now Sainte Petersburg), because a prosthetics institute was located there. I also studied in the Volgograd and Orlovsky Oblsasts in Russia. After graduating high school I enrolled into bookkeeping course at a college in Zagorsk, in the Moscow oblast and graduated it in 1987.

MEMOIRS

An anti-nuclear movement Nevada-Semipalatinsk was established in 1989 under the leadership of Kazakhstan's people's poet and writer Olzhas Suleimenov. I was an active member of that movement since joining it from day one. Suleimenov had the charisma to inspire millions of Kazakhs to follow him in the cause to shut down the nuclear test site in Kazakhstan that has brought suffering and mothers's tears on the Kazakh soil. In the 1990s I also took an active part in the struggle against nuclear tests by participating in rallies and protests at the polygons in Kazakhstan and the US. Our voices were heard by the President of Kazakhstan and a decree to shut down the Semipalatinsk nuclear test polygon was one of the first global anti-nuclear initiatives signed by President Nazarbayev on August 29, 1991.

When looking at the pictures of those days and recovering distant memories I can tell that my life has been full of bright people and heartbreaking moments. Among those stories is my encounter with the leader of an aboriginal tribe şoşon at the Nevada polygon. The man fell to his knees and spoke to the earth. I asked a translator what was going on with him and was told that the man was asking forgiveness from mother earth for the damage it had sustained from humans. The story has touched me profoundly and I remember the day as clear as today.

Another touching moment happened in Colorado when I was visiting school children of one of the schools. I told them about the sick children in Yegindybulak, my hometown, told them about the horrors those kids had faced throughout the years. That day the little American school children went home sad. But the next day they brought various first aid items like bandages, vitamins et cetera to ship to Kazakhstan. It was very emotional and moving. It was symbolic and uniting to know that the children had felt the pain of their peers - tens of thousands of kilometers away on the other side of the planet.

In 1990, on August 6 we travelled to Hiroshima and I was giving a speech in front of the numerous Japanese audience. As part of that speech I mentioned that out intentions were of good will and we came with nothing to hide, I said that I wanted to show them my open palms to ensure they were empty and I explained that I just couldn't do it as I was born without arms. What happened next stunned everyone who was there -- thousands of Japanese stood up and showed me their open palms to show their good intentions towards me.

Moments like make me believe that my time wasn't in vain.

As part of the Nevada-Semipalatinsk I started painting with my feet and my mouth and have a series of various works depicting the pain and consequences of nuclear tests. My paintings were exhibited in the US, Japan, Germany, Turkey and in Kazakhstan.

Throughout the years I have worked with the ill-children in my district; hosted charity exhibitions, fund-raising to cure the children of Yegindybulak. In 1999 I was awarded Order